THE FIRST
21 YEARS OF
INDEPENDENT
TELEVISION

"It shall be the
duty of the Authority
to provide the
television broadcasting
services as a
public service for
disseminating
information, education
and entertainment"

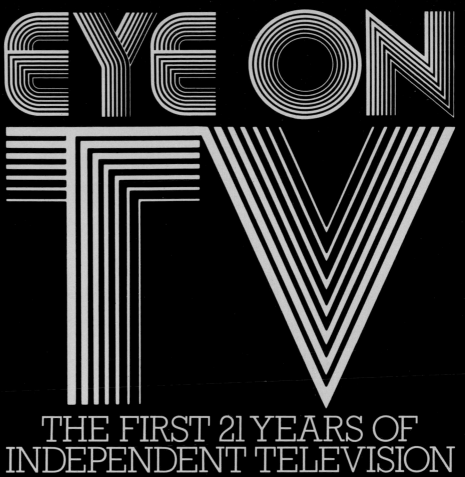

EYE ON TV

THE FIRST 21 YEARS OF INDEPENDENT TELEVISION

A TVTimes Book

Published by Independent Television Publications Limited
247 Tottenham Court Road, London W1P 0AU
© Independent Television Publications Limited 1976
ISBN Number 0 900727 61 6
Filmsetting by Text Typographics Limited, London
Printed and bound by Lund Humphries Limited, Bradford and London

INTRODUCTION

ITV came into being by 27 votes. That was the majority in the House of Commons on March 4, 1954, when the Television Bill – subsequently the Television Act – was passed. The Act empowered the Independent Television Authority, now the Independent Broadcasting Authority, "to provide television services additional to those of the BBC and of high quality."

In 1955, the first issue of TV Times promised: "So far television in this country has been a monopoly restricted by limited finance and often, or so it seemed, restricted by a lofty attitude towards the viewers by those in control. That situation has now undergone a great and dramatic change. Viewers will no longer have to accept what has been deemed best for them. The new Independent Television programme planners aim at giving viewers what viewers want..."

How well the planners achieved their aim was reflected in the audience figures. A year before ITV began – it was introduced by Leslie Mitchell at 7.15pm on September 22, 1955 – there were little more than 3.2 million licence holders; five years later, when all the major ITV stations had opened, the number was 9.2 million, and most people watched ITV.

For a time it was fashionable for public figures and leader writers to deride ITV for its popular programmes. "No one likes ITV – except the viewers," became an aphorism in television. But viewers did prefer ITV and it continues to be Britain's favourite television service.

As charged by the original Television Act, ITV pro-

vides "information, education and entertainment." On average, an ITV company transmits 100 hours of television a week. Of this, some 35 per cent is news, current affairs, documentaries, arts, religion and education; 24 per cent is drama; 10 per cent films; 12 per cent entertainment and music; 11 per cent sport, and eight per cent children's programmes.

This book recalls in pictures and words some of the highlights of the first 21 years of Britain's favourite channel. Not just information and education but the entertainment, too; not just the great and award-winning programmes but also fun shows. All have been part of the ITV story over the past 21 years.

CONTENTS

1955

ITV opened on September 22, after four years of argument. During this time, its advocates had decried BBC programmes as cosy and low budget, while its opponents had pointed to the American system and warned that commercial television would bring a lowering of standards in Britain.

But the Television Act of 1954 had set up the Independent Television Authority under Sir Kenneth– now Lord–Clark, Chairman of the Arts Council. And the ITA had devised a regional structure for ITV, and appointed programme companies.

Sir Winston Churchill, who had backed the alternative service, had handed over the Premiership to Sir Anthony Eden by the time it started, while Clement Attlee was about to be succeeded as Labour leader by Hugh Gaitskell.

ITV's impact was immediate. The public were fascinated by its newscasters, cash quiz shows, American programmes, and commercials.

But ITV was available only in the London area, and by the end of the year reached a mere 12.5 per cent of the homes in the country.

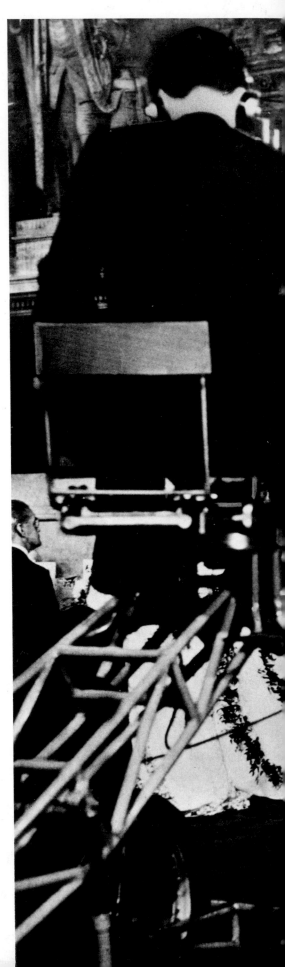

ITV was officially opened at 7.15pm on September 22, when a dinner to mark the occasion was transmitted from the Guildhall, London. Speeches to welcome the new service were made by Sir Kenneth Clark; the Lord Mayor, Sir Seymour Howard; and the Postmaster General, Dr. Charles Hill, later Chairman successively of the ITA and BBC.

The Scarlet Pimpernel was among ITV's early programmes to prove popular. Marius Goring starred as Baroness Orczy's swashbuckling hero. (Associated-Rediffusion)

ITV launched big-name variety in its first week, with **Sunday Night at the London Palladium.** The show was compered by Tommy Trinder, starred Gracie Fields, and featured The Tiller Girls. (ATV)

The Adventures of Robin Hood, with Richard Greene in the title role, was to become one of television's most successful film series. (ATV)

The first commercial was transmitted at 8.12 on opening night when an urgent voice proclaimed: "It's tingling fresh, it's fresh as ice...it's Gibbs SR toothpaste."

Former bandleader Jack Jackson introduced **Variety,** a programme for opening night which presented "some of the stars who will be featured regularly on ITV..." Among them were Reg Dixon and Harry Secombe. (ATV)

Boris Karloff played **Col. March of Scotland Yard** in a crime series about the Yard's "Department of Queer Complaints". (ATV)

Chris Chataway (24), the record-breaking athlete, read ITN's first news at 10pm on September 22. He was the newscaster for their main programmes. (ITN)

Margaret Leighton,
Sir John Gielgud and
Dame Edith Evans
appeared in a scene
from **The Importance
of Being Earnest,**
one of three excerpts
from plays on ITV's
gala inaugural night.
(Associated-
Rediffusion)

13

Godfrey Winn invited viewers to write to him about their domestic problems; these were scripted and presented with his solutions in **As Others See Us.** (Associated-Rediffusion)

Fanny's Kitchen was the title of ITV's first cookery series. Although it was presented by Fanny Cradock—assisted in later series by husband Johnny— she was introduced as Phyllis Cradock. (Associated-Rediffusion)

Michaela and Armand Denis were the stars of ITV's first wildlife series, which they filmed in Africa. (ATV)

Double Your Money, Hughie Green's cash quiz, was to become one of the most popular programmes on ITV. (Associated-Rediffusion)

Michael Miles introduced his first **Take Your Pick** quiz show – complete with "yes-no" interlude – on ITV's second night. (Associated-Rediffusion)

15

Mick and Montmorency
starred in a series of
15-minute comedy
programmes; behind
the pseudonyms
were Charlie Drake
and Jack Edwardes.
(Associated-
Rediffusion)

Actor-turned-produce
Douglas Fairbank
introduced the first i
his series of IT
dramas, **Dougla
Fairbanks Present**
(Associated
Rediffusion

ITV introduced **Free Speech**, political cross-talk between Sir Robert (now Lord) Boothby, W. J. Brown, Michael Foot and A. J. P. Taylor. The new programme was similar to the BBC's **In the News**, in which the four appeared. This had been dropped when the main political parties attempted to substitute orthodox representatives. Boxing promoter Jack Solomons introduced action from big fights in **Jack Solomons' Scrapbook**.

ITV's first daily serial was **Sixpenny Corner**, a 15-minute drama shown weekday mornings. It starred Patricia Dainton and Howard Pays as garage owners. Popular American programmes on ITV included the crime series **Dragnet**, the comedy **I Love Lucy**, and the Westerns **Gun Law** and **Hopalong Cassidy**.

1956

ITV spread to the Midlands and North, and by the end of the year was in more than a quarter of the homes in the country. Its programmes topped the ratings, but advertisers were still wary of spending £1,000 a minute on the new medium while its coverage was still somewhat limited.

Understandably, many ITV programmes were dedicated to mass entertainment; only 19 per cent of the output was classed by the ITA as "serious".

ATV took the initiative in obtaining permission from the Postmaster General to show religious programmes between 6 and 7.30 on Sunday evenings, when television had been shut down in order not to deter churchgoing. The first programme was **About Religion**, a series of interviews.

The Postmaster General also revoked the notorious Fourteen Day Rule, which had barred TV from discussing controversial subjects due for Parliamentary debate during the following fortnight.

Nasser seized the Suez Canal and Prime Minister Eden ordered an invasion of Egypt. Russia sent tanks to Hungary to crush demands for democracy.

Boyd QC, ITV's first courtroom drama series, was created by Jack Roffey and illustrated many facets of trials justice. It was so accurate that Michael Denison, who played the "silk", received invitations to address Law Society dinners…
(Associated-Rediffusion)

1956

Among the many quiz shows of the period, **The 64,000 Question** was derived from an American series. The British show featured Jerry Desmonde as quizmaster and ex-Det. Supt. Robert Fabian was "custodian of the questions". (ATV)

The Adventures of Sir Lancelot concerned the legendary knights of King Arthur's round table. William Russell played the romantic hero. (ATV)

Brian Inglis was a frequent presenter of **What the Papers Say,** TV's weekly survey of how Fleet Street has treated the news. (Granada)

McDonald Hobley introduced **Yakity-Yak,** a panel game that would attract little support from the Women's Lib group. It was subtitled "the dizzy show" and encouraged the six girl panellists to give silly answers to the questions. (ATV)

1956

The Count of Monte Cristo, a series based on the Dumas story, starred George Dolenz as the Count. (ATV)

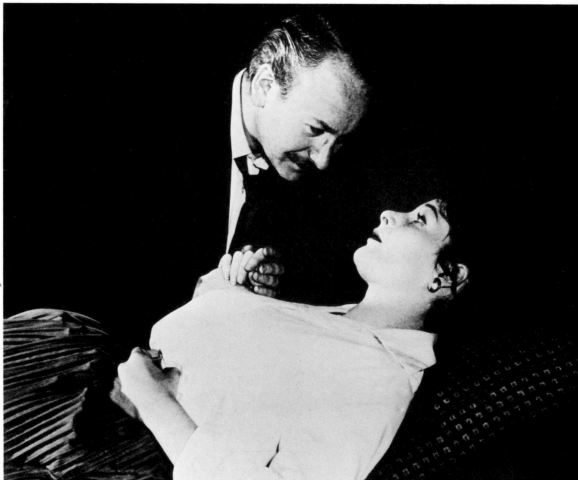

Plays of this period were usually adapted from stage successes, as there was no corps of established playwrights. **The Outsider,** first of the **Armchair Theatre** productions, was adapted from the 1923 Dorothy Brandon drama about medical ethics, and starred Adrienne Corri and David Kossoff. (ABC)

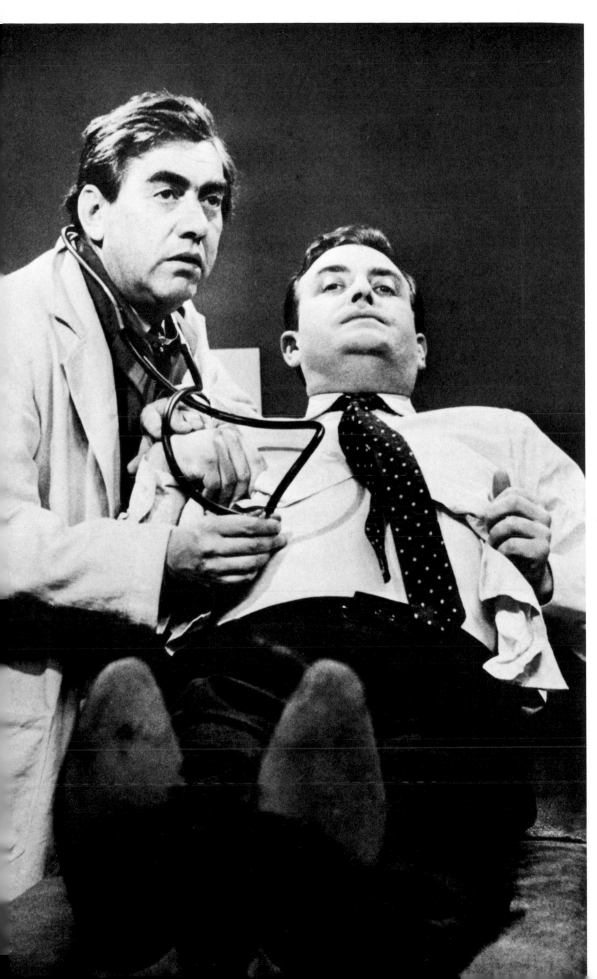

Ludovic Kennedy's long association with ITV began when he was invited to replace Chris Chataway as one of ITN's regular newscasters. (ITN)

After his spectacular success on BBC Radio, comic Tony Hancock transferred his talents to television. **The Tony Hancock Show** was the first of many series he made for ITV. (Associated-Rediffusion)

Sport was still comparatively sparse on television, but in **Jack Solomons' Scrapbook,** the fight promoter showed film of famous bouts. In 1956 – the year when Rocky Marciano retired as undefeated World Heavyweight Champion – Solomons recalled Marciano's defeat of Archie Moore the previous year. (ATV)

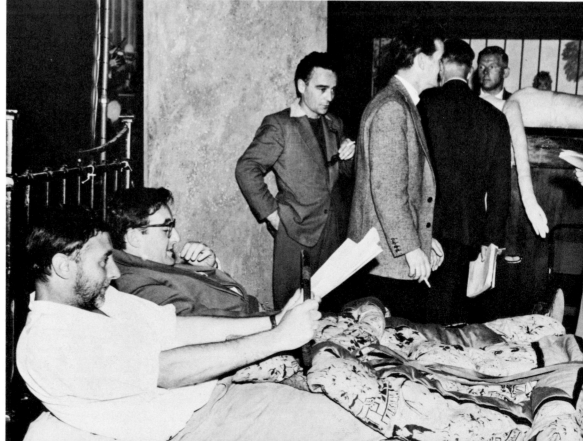

The Goons brought a new and anarchic humour to radio; with **Son of Fred,** Spike Milligan and Peter Sellers made an early attempt to do the same on television. (Associated-Rediffusion)

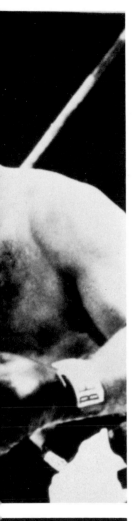

Catherine Boyle appeared in a panel game, **I've Got a Secret!** Here she was inaugurating a studio switchboard with a call to Ben Lyon, Chairman of the programme. (Associated-Rediffusion)

Robert Shaw played a swashbuckling, ex-pirate captain in **The Buccaneers,** and was hailed as "one of the most exciting romantic discoveries of the year." (ATV)

25

Stealing scenes from Arthur Askey isn't easy, but Sabrina did so in **Before Your Very Eyes**; her vital statistics caused nationwide comment. (Associated-Rediffusion)

Domestic comedies featuring real-life husband and wife teams were popular on TV at this time. Among them was **My Husband and I**, starring Evelyn Laye and Frank Lawton. (Associated-Rediffusion)

In **The Arthur Haynes Show**, written by Johnny Speight, the comedian appeared regularly as a tramp who discomfited authority. (ATV)

The future star of **Crossroads** introduced her own series, **Tea With Noele Gordon,** in which she talked to guests about life in the theatre. The Guild of Television Producers and Directors voted ITN newscaster Chris Chataway the TV Personality of the year. **This Week** began, packing as many as six contrasting items into 30 minutes. Hughie Green introduced **Opportunity Knocks!** which had been a radio favourite for many years. Among the new shows from America were **The Errol Flynn Theatre,** and **Highway Patrol,** starring Broderick Crawford. This series gave rise to the catchphrase "Ten-four," Crawford's acknowledgement of radio messages. Comedy stars with their own series included Alfred Marks, Joan and Leslie Randall, Dora Bryan, rubber-faced Libby Morris, and Bernard Braden and Barbara Kelly. **My Wildest Dream** featured Marks, David Nixon, Tommy Trinder and Terry-Thomas.

1957

In the year Harold Macmillan replaced Anthony Eden as Premier–and went on to launch the era of "You've never had it so good"–the finances of ITV began to improve. As ITV spread into central Scotland, the revenue of the pioneer companies increased, though their losses were to total £11 million in the first 18 months.

Although determined never to lose contact with the mass audience, ITV became the first channel to screen programmes for schools. It also introduced outside broadcasts of Sunday morning church services, beginning with a Battle of Britain drumhead service from RAF, Biggin Hill.

The "toddlers' truce"–a shutdown of both ITV and BBC Television between 6 pm and 7 pm so mothers could put small children to bed–came to an end.

And on Saturday nights, television continued until midnight. The extra hour was used to show a feature film. A combined TV and radio licence went up by £1 to £4.

Emergency-Ward 10, a twice-weekly serial about hospital life, began a successful 10-year run, and won a production award from the Guild of Television Producers and Directors. (ATV)

Cooper–Life With Tommy, introduced the comic conjurer in his own series. It was the beginning of an association with ITV that has continued. (Associated-Rediffusion)

The interview which Robin Day conducted with President Nasser in Cairo was one of the most significant to date. It took place soon after the Suez crisis, while Britain was still technically at war with Egypt. Day was Guild of Television Producers and Directors' TV Personality of the Year. (ITN)

Making his debut in **Murder Bag,** Det. Insp. Tom Lockhart, played by Raymond Francis, went on to appear in **No Hiding Place.** In the 10-year period, he rose to the rank of Chief Superintendent. (Associated-Rediffusion)

31

1957

Lunch Box, a music show with Noele Gordon as hostess, introduced in the Midlands at the end of 1956, achieved recognition when it was shown on the network. (ATV)

The first quiz show with a noughts and crosses formula was Criss Cross Quiz, introduced by Jeremy Hawk. (Granada)

Actor John Slater introduced one of the first advertising magazines, **Slater's Bazaar,** in which commercials were interwoven with light entertainment. (ATV)

Mark Saber was one of the first British series to be sold to America. It starred Donald Gray as a one-armed detective. (ATV)

To celebrate a visit to Paris by the Queen, London and the French capital were linked by **Telerama.** Showbusiness stars were introduced by Leslie Mitchell in London and Art Buchwald in Paris. (Associated-Rediffusion)

Eighty schools viewed **Looking and Seeing,** the first programme for schools. The new service resulted from the initiative of Paul Adorian, the Managing Director of Associated-Rediffusion.

Theatre techniques, with close-ups of actors in the studio, were used in the production of **Shadow Squad,** a series starring Rex Garner as a Flying Squad officer turned private crimebuster. (Associated-Rediffusion)

Former Goons Peter Sellers and Michael Bentine joined forces for the zany comedy series, **Yes, It's the Cathode-Ray Tube Show.** (Associated-Rediffusion)

Jim's Inn, the most popular advertising magazine, featured Jimmy Hanley as the landlord of a village pub. These magazines were to be banned by Parliament in 1963. (Associated-Rediffusion)

Another quiz show of the year was **Bury Your Hatchet,** in which couples with a grudge against each other competed for money prizes. The hosts were Bob Monkhouse and Denis Goodwin. (ATV)

The Army Game was destined to become one of ITV's biggest situation comedy successes. William Hartnell played the CSM. (Granada)

Sir Ivone Kirkpatrick, former Permanent Under Secretary of State at the Foreign Office, succeeded Sir Kenneth Clark as Chairman of the ITA. For the first time, the Queen made her traditional Christmas Day broadcast on television.

John Grierson, acknowledged father of the documentary film, wrote and introduced **This Wonderful World**, which examined documentary films from all over the world. The series – it continued until 1966 – was the new Scottish Television's first regular contribution to the network.

Huw Thomas, who had joined ITN's newscasting team at the end of 1956, established himself as a popular ITV personality.

The first successful videotape recorders were imported from America. Television, until now live or on film, would soon be able to record programmes for showing at a later date. Studios could be employed around the clock, and artists appear whenever they were available.

1958

Television finally superseded radio as the more popular home entertainment. This development was helped by ITV's expansion into South Wales, the West and Southern England. There were now 6.5 million homes with ITV reception.

As ITV gained confidence in holding the mass audience, it extended its range to include new arts programmes and original drama productions.

Political discussion on television had always ceased when an election campaign began, for fear of accusations that voters were being influenced. But while the BBC followed the accepted practice for the Rochdale by-election, Granada—after taking eminent legal advice—gave the campaign major coverage, and opened the way for today's comprehensive election coverage.

Nikita Khruschev took over in the Kremlin and Pope John in the Vatican. Pictures of the Pope's installation were transmitted live via Eurovision. Iceland extended her territorial fishing limits to 12 miles.

Fred Robinson created **The Larkins** for Scout concerts, but the Cockney family soon became national favourites when they were introduced to television. Peggy Mount and David Kossoff played Ada and Alf Larkin in the series. (ATV)

1958

The Sunday Break, the brainchild of Howard Thomas, then Managing Director of ABC, was the first "pop" religious show. Set in a youth club, with pop music in the background, it posed questions of interest to young people. (ABC)

Diana Dors and Alan Melville were among artists living or working in the South who were featured in **Southern Rhapsody,** a gala programme on the opening night of Southern Television.

Jackie Rae posed the questions, Marion Ryan was the resident singer, in **Spot the Tune.** (Granada)

People in Trouble, from kleptomaniacs to alcoholics, were interviewed by Dan Farson, labelled ITV's "Mr. Documentary". (Associated-Rediffusion)

Bruce Forsyth joined **Sunday Night at the London Palladium** as compere – direct from pierhead shows. He was the first artist to achieve stardom via this job. (ATV)

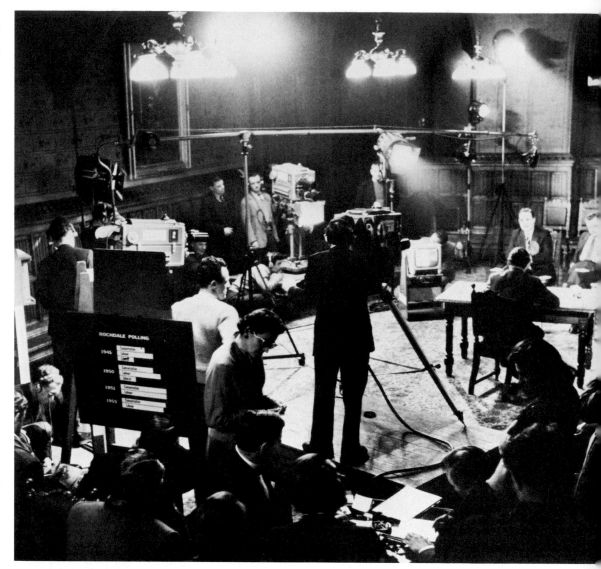

ITV presented its
first coverage of an
election campaign
at the Rochdale
by-election. Voters
were interviewed
in the streets and
the candidates
allotted equal studio
time. (Granada)

The Outside Broadcast
cameras introduced
an unfamiliar sport
when they showed
Prince Philip playing
in a polo match
in Windsor Great Park.
(Associated-
Rediffusion)

Television returned to the Classics with the adventure series **Ivanhoe,** starring Roger Moore, described at the time as "practically unknown". (ATV)

The ventriloquist Peter Brough introduced a new, walking Archie Andrews dummy when **Educating Archie** was moved from radio to television. Dick Emery was one of the regular cast. (Associated-Rediffusion)

The Verdict is Yours, a series of mock trials, had plots but no scripts. Actors playing witnesses and counsel improvised their lines. (Granada)

Granada Television maintained a film unit at London Zoo for their natural history programmes. Among them was **Zoo Time,** presented by Desmond Morris, then the Curator of Mammals. (Granada)

1958

One of the most popular comedians in the country was Dave King, a regular celebrity in **Val Parnell's Saturday Spectacular.** (ATV)

Robert Beatty starred as a tough Canadian Mountie attached to Scotland Yard in **Dial 999**, a crime series aimed at the valuable American market. (ATV)

The State opening of Parliament by the Queen was televised for the first time. Robin Day was the commentator for ITV.

The Queen, accompanied by Prince Philip, paid her first visit to ITA's headquarters, then at Princes Gate, Kensington. Jack Good produced **Oh Boy!** ITV's first pop show for teenagers. There were major developments in ITV's coverage of the arts. **The Book Man** was the first television series devoted entirely to writers and their works. Sir Kenneth Clark presented a series entitled **Is Art Necessary?** Laurence Olivier made his television debut in Henrik Ibsen's **John Gabriel Borkman.** Many programmes were still transmitted live at this time. Among them were the **Armchair Theatre** plays. During the broadcast of **Underground,** one of the cast collapsed and died. While out of camera shot, the other actors were told that he had been taken ill and they would have to improvise; they carried on.

1959

The first General Election to be covered fully by television – due to ITV's innovatory coverage of the 1958 Rochdale by-election – returned Harold Macmillan to Downing Street for another term.

ITV expanded into North East England, East Anglia and Northern Ireland to reach a total of 8.6 million homes, more than 55 per cent of all those in the British Isles. By this time, ITV was watched by 70 per cent of those with a choice of viewing, and by June the ITA had repaid the £555,000 borrowed from the Postmaster General to start operations.

Fidel Castro seized power in Cuba, and civil war broke out in the Belgian Congo. Russia and America began training astronauts. At home, the first stretch of the M1 Motorway was opened.

Holiday Town Parade, a combined bathing beauty, fashion queen and male Adonis contest, with heats in seaside resorts, was shown on the national network after three years in the Midlands and North. (ABC)

Ed Murrow, the noted American journalist, spoke on the merits and defects of television in the first televised **Granada Lecture** at London's Guildhall. (Granada)

To mark the centenary of Isambard Kingdom Brunel's death, Peter Wyngarde portrayed him in the dramatised documentary, **Engineer Extraordinary.** (TWW)

Probation Officer was applauded for its authenticity: an episode on the after-care of prisoners was shown to members of both Houses of Parliament during the passage of the controversial Criminal Justice Bill. (ATV)

John Turner starred in **Knight Errant,** a drama series about a modern crusader who championed the oppressed. (Granada)

1959

International stars Vittorio de Sica, Jack Hawkins, Dan Dailey and Richard Conte played **The Four Just Men** in a series based on the Edgar Wallace thriller. (ATV)

Domestic sketches, song and dance were the ingredients of **The Dickie Henderson Half Hour,** with Anthea Askey playing his wife. (Associated-Rediffusion)

Many celebrated actors and actresses were now making their TV debuts; here, Vivien Leigh was Sabina in Thornton Wilder's **The Skin of Our Teeth.** (Granada)

1959

As the airlines began regular jet services, ITV launched **Skyport,** a drama series about the activities at an international airport. (Granada)

Alun Owen won the Guild of TV Producers and Directors' award for Best Scriptwriter, helped by his first TV play, **No Tram to Lime Street,** an **Armchair Theatre** play starring Jack Hedley and Billie Whitelaw. She was the Guild's TV Actress of the Year. (ABC)

Land of Song meant, of course, Wales and featured Welsh choirs and singers. Ivor Emmanuel was the star of this long running series. (TWW)

Bernard Braden and Huw Thomas introduced **Let's Go,** the first Saturday afternoon programme to visit sporting events around the country. Sir John Gielgud appeared in **A Day By the Sea** and Flora Robson in **Mother Courage.**
Mary Holland made her debut as Katie, the pretty housewife preparing lunch for her good-natured husband, Philip, in the Oxo commercials.
New American Westerns included **Have Gun – Will Travel,** starring Richard Boone.

1960

A committee under the chairmanship of Sir Harry Pilkington, the glass manufacturer, was set up to consider the future of broadcasting. Meanwhile, ITV extended into South East England and sales of its programmes abroad began to grow.

In the first year of the so-called Swinging Sixties, viewers saw TV confrontations swing it for John F. Kennedy in the United States presidential election. Princess Margaret married photographer Antony Armstrong-Jones. The courts freed Lady Chatterley's Lover for publication, and the News of the World serialised the memoirs of actress Diana Dors.

Coronation Street began – and the hair-netted, vinegary Ena Sharples, played by Violet Carson, was soon established as one of ITV's greatest characters ever. (Granada)

Jean Clarke wiggled to stardom as one of the hostesses on **Double Your Money.** She said of her eye-catching walk: "I just can't help it." (Associated-Rediffusion)

Ingenious hoaxes such as this baffled victims of **Candid Camera.** Their various reactions were recorded by hidden cameras. (ABC)

The largest number of ITV cameras ever assembled for one event covered the wedding of Princess Margaret and Antony Armstrong-Jones.

Danger Man, one of ITV's most successful adventure series, starred Patrick McGoohan as a tough, globetrotting security agent. (ATV)

Arthur Christiansen, ex-Editor of the Daily Express, was editorial adviser to **Deadline Midnight,** a drama series set in Fleet Street. (ATV)

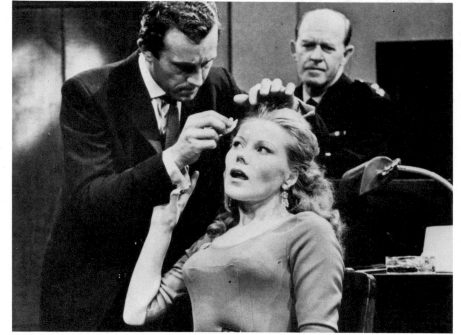

Ian Hendry played Dr. Geoffrey Brent in the drama series **Police Surgeon.** One year later, Hendry starred as the same character in the first of **The Avengers** series. (ABC)

The Canadian couple Barbara Kelly and Bernard Braden were in demand for many types of show. Here, they were appearing as themselves in the new comedy series **Rolling Stones.** (ATV)

Our House, a comedy series by **Carry On** film writer Norman Hudis, featured a boarding house and its bizarre group of residents. (ABC)

Moira Lister was the star of **Flotsam and Jetsam,** the first in the series **Somerset Maugham Hour.** (Associated-Rediffusion)

The Royal Variety
Performance was
televised for the
first time. The
Queen and Prince
Philip were amused
particularly by
the Crazy Gang, who
were to become
regular favourites
in the show. (ATV)

63

1960

The Derby was shown throughout Britain for the first time. ITV viewers watched Lester Piggott romp home on St. Paddy. (Associated-Rediffusion)

The Strange World of Gurney Slade was a whimsical rarity in television comedy. Surrounded by lovely girls, Anthony Newley spoke to trees and animals – and they answered. (ATV)

An early example of a "spin-off," **Bootsie and Snudge** followed **The Army Game**'s Bill Fraser and Alfie Bass into civilian life. (Granada)

Margot Fonteyn and Michael Somes danced in the Royal Ballet's production of Frederick Ashton's **Cinderella**. The television studio gave double the space of the stage at Covent Garden. (Granada)

The comedy series **Mess Mates** was set on a small cargo ship plying around Britain's coast. (Associated-Rediffusion)

The props department acquired genuine Victorian draper's trimmings for the eight-part series **Kipps,** adapted from H.G. Wells' novel by Clive Exton, and starring Brian Murray. (Granada)

Our Street, a seven-part documentary, examined life in a typical working class road in Camberwell, South East London. (Associated-Rediffusion)

Sunday Night at the London Palladium had become a national institution. Vicars even altered the times of evening services so the congregations could watch the show. Average audiences numbered 17 million, but Cliff Richard won 19.5 million, Max Bygraves 21 million, and Harry Secombe 22 million.

Diana Dors made her ITV drama debut in an **Armchair Theatre** play called **The Innocent**.

American imports included **77 Sunset Strip**, and the Western **Bonanza**. **Biggles**, W. E. Johns' story for children about a flying ace, was adapted for television.

Twenty Questions, the animal, vegetable and mineral quiz, moved to ITV under the chairmanship of Stewart MacPherson.

1961

The television industry was concerned with technical questions regarding its future. An international conference allocated new UHF frequencies, making it possible for Britain to have new channels in addition to the existing ones on VHF. Other conferences sought in vain to agree on a common system of colour.

But the Government decided that colour should not be introduced until a third channel was in existence – on UHF – and the Continental 625 line standard had begun to replace the 405 line system.

Meanwhile, ITV expanded into South West England, North East Scotland and the Borders. The number of ITV homes rose to 11.3 million.

Current affairs and documentary programmes reflected a fast changing world – the first spaceman, Russia's Yuri Gagarin; the building of the Berlin Wall; South Africa becoming a republic, and Britain's application to join the Common Market.

The first programme in the award-winning natural history series, **Survival,** dealt with London's wildlife, including Hampstead Heath's fox families. (Anglia)

1961

The **Avengers** began, with Ian Hendry as a doctor and Patrick Macnee an umbrella-wielding secret agent; the lovely, lethal judo girls were yet to make a debut. (ABC)

Set in a fictional London department store, **Harpers West One** was a drama series featuring Jan Holden. (ATV)

Family Solicitor attracted praise from the Law Society, who said: "For years we have waited for television to present a series like this." (Granada)

1961

Without referring to maps or notes, A. J. P. Taylor delivered a highly praised series of lectures on the **First World War.** (ATV)

Sammy Davis Jr., now at the height of his popularity, came to Britain to star in **Sunday Night at the London Palladium**, and **Sammy Davis Meets the Girls**. (ATV)

The Earl of Harewood, Edinburgh Festival's Artistic Director, introduced the weekly arts series, **Tempo**, which was edited by Kenneth Tynan. (ABC)

The trial of Soviet spies Peter and Helen Kroger, who were sentenced to 20 years imprisonment in the Portland secrets case, was followed by a documentary, **35 Cranley Drive.** (Granada)

The Quiet War, an incisive look at the guerilla struggle in Vietnam, was a British contribution to a series of films made for world-wide showing by Intertel. (Associated-Rediffusion)

Although renowned for realistic, modern drama, **Armchair Theatre** screened an award-winning fantasy on the theme of beauty and the beast, Alun Owen's **The Rose Affair**. (ABC)

1961

As America backed a military invasion to overthrow Cuba's Fidel Castro, ITV screened four documentaries about the country, entitled **Cuba...Si!** (Granada)

The trial of former Gestapo chief Adolf Eichmann, accused of crimes against humanity, took place in Jerusalem and was shown exclusively in Britain on ITV. (ATV)

The Duke of Kent's marriage to Katharine Worsley brought scenes of splendour to York Minster. Nine ITV commentators described the event.

The first in a series of exchange television programmes with Russia was the live transmission of the British Trade Fair opening in Moscow's Sokolniki Park.
An early documentary in the series **Into Europe** asked: "Will farmers survive if Britain joins the Common Market?"
The Inauguration of John F. Kennedy as President of the United States was shown in a one-hour programme the following day.
William Franklyn – not yet associated with the Schw... commercials – starred as a British agent in South America in **Top Secret**.

1962

There were significant developments in television news. Telstar, the first satellite capable of relaying television across the Atlantic, was launched and British viewers saw the first live pictures from America.

And when President Kennedy confronted Khrushchev in the week-long Cuban missiles crisis, it was to television that Britons turned to discover whether it was to be peace or war. By the end of the year, television was the main source of news for 52 per cent of the population – double the figure in 1957.

The Pilkington Committee's report approved the BBC's television service but was critical of some aspects of ITV. The Government rejected the Committee's recommendation that the ITA should take over the planning of schedules and selling of advertising, but it awarded the third channel to the BBC.

Meanwhile, ITV moved into North and West Wales, the Channel Isles and Ulster to become available to 96 per cent of the population.

Thalidomide was withdrawn after causing deformities in babies, Britain and France agreed to build a supersonic airliner, Concorde.

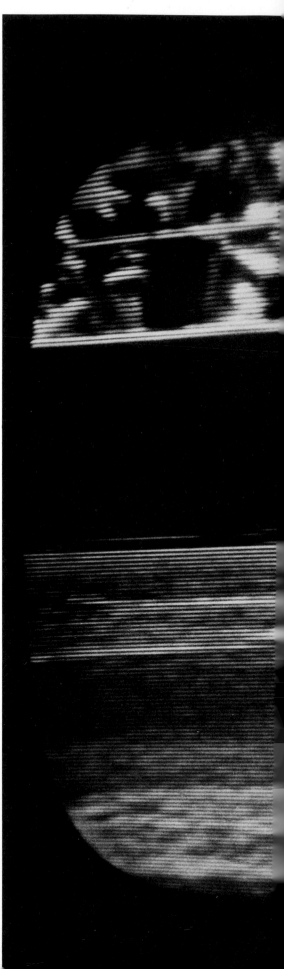

First transmissions via the new American satellite, Telstar, showed baseball from Chicago, an excerpt from a production of **Macbeth** in Ontario, and a Presidential press conference in Washington. (ITN)

The Piraikon Greek
Tragedy Theatre
Company performed
Electra, the 2,500-year-
old play by Sophocles…
in their native tongue.
(Associated-
Rediffusion)

The hero of **Man of the World** was a photo journalist, played by Craig Stevens, which gave an opportunity to dress the female characters in chic clothes designed by the Fashion House Group. (ATV)

Norman Vaughan was Bruce Forsyth's successor as compere of **Sunday Night at the London Palladium** and delighted audiences with funny mannerisms and the catchphrases "dodgy" and "swinging". (ATV)

For years, Eric Morecambe and Ernie Wise have ended their shows with a running gag. In **The Morecambe and Wise Show** – written by Dick Hills and Sid Green – they always attempted to leave the stage by a door that was too small. (ATV)

1962

University Challenge was one of the most demanding quiz shows to date. Offering no individual prizes, it featured teams of students answering questions posed by the erudite Bamber Gascoigne. (Granada)

The Saint, based on the character created by Leslie Charteris, came to ITV as a series of hour-long thrillers, with Roger Moore starring in the title role. It ran for seven years and was sold to 80 countries. (ATV)

Armchair Theatre commissioned Robert Muller's first play, **Afternoon of a Nymph,** with Janet Munro playing a film starlet and Ian Hendry as a director. (ABC)

A new comedy series written by Jack Rosenthal and Harry Driver, **Bulldog Breed** starred Donald Churchill as Tom Bowler, an engaging young man with a gift for creating chaos. (Granada)

1962

Short stories by **Saki**
(H. H. Munro) were
adapted as a series
for television and
played by a company
which included
husky-voiced Fenella
Fielding. (Granada)

Honor Blackman joined **The Avengers** as attractive judo girl Mrs. Cathy Gale – and caused a fashion sensation with her leather suits and high boots. (ABC)

The Guild of Television Producers and Directors conferred a special award for news programmes on Geoffrey Cox, Editor of ITN. Ballet idol Rudolf Nureyev topped the bill of **Sunday Night at the London Palladium.** Prince Philip appeared in **This Week** to report on his tour of South America. A TWW programme on **Dylan Thomas** won a Hollywood Motion Picture Academy award as the best short subject documentary. **Thank Your Lucky Stars** won an award from Melody Maker magazine as the best TV pop show. A new quiz show with a crossword puzzle formula was **Take a Letter,** with Robert Holness as Chairman.

1963

The nation was gripped by Beatlemania but, following the Pilkington Committee's strictures, ITV increased the proportion of programmes classed as "serious" by the ITA to 37 per cent.

The wider range included the first adult education on British TV, with Sunday morning lessons in English and French, and a new current affairs series, **World in Action,** was introduced.

Lord Hill of Luton, the wartime radio doctor, succeeded Sir Ivone Kirkpatrick as Chairman of the ITA. Harold Macmillan yielded the Premiership to Sir Alec Douglas-Home. Harold Wilson became leader of the Labour party on the death of Hugh Gaitskell. War Minister John Profumo resigned, Pope John died, and President Kennedy was assassinated.

His funeral was shown live in Britain via Early Bird, successor to Telstar and the first satellite to remain stationary and be available for use at all times.

Beginning as a drama series concerning shopfloor workers in an aircraft factory, **The Plane Makers** was soon preoccupied with boardroom politics. Patrick Wymark played the ruthless Managing Director, John Wilder, who was the prototype for a variety of modern anti-heroes. (ATV)

1963

Central character in
The Human Jungle
was a psychiatrist,
played by Herbert
Lom, whose readiness
to become involved
in his patients'
problems provided
the basis for a
unique series. (ABC)

Spies, secret agents, saboteurs and undercover men were the heroes of **Espionage,** a series of 26 self-contained dramas. (ATV)

The first series of **Our Man at St. Mark's** starred Leslie Phillips as the vicar. Donald Sinden later took the role. (Associated-Rediffusion)

Men of Our Time was a documentary series that examined world leaders of the 20th century. Included was an assessment by James Cameron of Mahatma Gandhi, the passive revolutionary who founded present-day India. (Granada)

The Victorians, eight
plays originally
presented on stage in
the 19th century,
was performed by the
Company of Seven,
a TV repertory group
assembled for
the series. (Granada)

Few plays have won the honours accorded to **The Lover,** a stylish sex comedy by Harold Pinter. It brought him The Guild of Television Producers and Directors' Best Script award, while Vivien Merchant and Alan Badel were the Guild's Best Actress and Actor, and director Joan Kemp–Welch won the Desmond Davis award for outstanding creative work. The play also won the coveted Prix Italia. (Associated-Rediffusion)

The urge to get away was exploited by **Crane,** an adventure series about a Briton, played by Patrick Allen, who gave up his job to run a cafe, a boat and a smuggling business in Morocco. (Associated-Rediffusion)

Love Story was an example of the trend away from single plays to anthologies. The series' common theme was romance, involving all classes and ages. Roger Livesey appeared in the leading role in **Raymond's Italian Woman**; Lea Padovani was the object of his affections. (ATV)

1963

ITV's biggest outside broadcast since the marriage of Princess Margaret was another royal wedding, that of Princess Alexandra to the Hon. Angus Ogilvy. Brian Connell was the commentator in Westminster Abbey and a total of 29 TV cameras was used.

The compelling style of **World in Action** was due largely to producer Tim Hewat. An early programme, **High Fashion**, looked at the haute couture industry. (Granada)

The world mourned the death of John F. Kennedy, whose promising presidency was ended by an assassin's bullet. The funeral was given special ITV coverage.

On the Braden Beat, a unique mixture of entertainment and investigations into consumer complaints, won Bernard Braden a Guild of Television Producers and Directors' award for performance in factual programmes. Geoffrey Cox, Editor of ITN, was honoured for the second year in succession, receiving the Television Society's silver medal for production.

A two-and-three-quarter hour production of **War and Peace,** with a cast of 40, won Granada an Emmy award.

Advertising magazines were banned by Parliament; commercials were subsequently confined to natural breaks.

A year after he had announced his retirement from show-business, Charlie Drake changed his mind and began a new comedy series, **The Charlie Drake Show.**

In response to viewer demand, Leonard White, the new producer of **Armchair Theatre,** moved away from "kitchen sink" drama to a policy of star names and popular plays.

1964

The Television Act extended the life of Independent Television – originally licensed for 10 years – to 1976, and gave the ITA increased powers over programmes and advertising.

Before deciding the programme contractors for the new period, the Authority interviewed 22 groups of applicants, including the existing contractors. It then reappointed the existing companies until 1967, by which time it hoped ITV would be operating the proposed fourth channel.

While the BBC began transmissions on its second, 625 line channel, a levy was imposed on ITV's advertising revenue. This achieved its object, cutting the profits of the programme companies and taking £22 million from them in 1964/5.

After a General Election in which he demonstrated unprecedented mastery of television by a politician, Harold Wilson became Premier. Meanwhile, Mods and Rockers rioted at the seaside, and pirate radio ships stole audiences from the BBC.

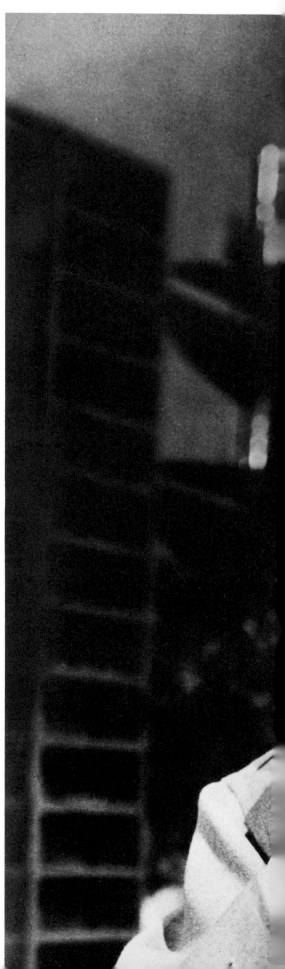

Crossroads, set in a country motel and starring Noele Gordon, was a Midlands triumph. Although it was shown four days a week in the area, it did not achieve national networking until 1972. (ATV)

1964

As Martin Luther King led civil rights marches in America, and won a Nobel Peace Prize, ITV screened a programme of negro protest songs called **Freedom Road,** which won all three major prizes at Berlin's Television Festival. (Associated-Rediffusion)

Sir Kenneth Clark toured **Great Temples of the World** and talked compellingly about both their architectural merits and history.
He is seen here at Karnak. (ATV)

To mark Britain's celebration of the 400th anniversary of Shakespeare's birth, ITV showed a production of **A Midsummer Night's Dream.** (Rediffusion)

1964

The face of the year was that of top model Jean Shrimpton. **A World in Action** camera crew trailed her on modelling assignments in New York and London for **The Face On the Cover.** (Granada)

Blackburn's Valerie Martin won the first Miss TVTimes contest, beating 5,000 contestants to take the crown in the final programme, **Glamour All the Way.** Adam Faith sang on the show and Patrick Macnee was one of the panel of star judges. (ABC)

Recalling memories of Will Hay's vintage comedy films, **Fire Crackers** concerned the antics of Cropper's End Fire Brigade and their circa 1907 fire appliance. (ATV)

Blithe Spirit, one of the series A Choice of Coward, starred Hattie Jacques as the medium, Madame Arcati, Joanna Dunham as the lovely, spectral Elvira. (Granada)

Derek Granger took over as presenter of Cinema from Bamber Gascoigne, who had launched this series of clips from films, and star interviews, three months earlier. (Granada)

With concern growing about the mounting number of accidents on the roads, **This Week** showed a shock programme in which Desmond Wilcox spoke to motorists as they left public houses. (Rediffusion)

The Other Man, by Giles Cooper, had a cast of 200 headed by Michael Caine. At 2 hrs. 20 min., it was ITV's longest-ever play. (Granada)

The comedy series **A Little Big Business** concerned a family furniture firm, with David Kossoff and Francis Matthews as argumentative father and son. (Granada)

105

Ted Willis devised **The Sullavan Brothers,** a series about four young lawyers, and promised: "We shall fire a few salvoes at British justice."(ATV)

The Celebrity Game, summer replacement for **Take Your Pick,** was a quiz in which contestants guessed celebrities' views on topical subjects. Among the guests was Groucho Marx. (Rediffusion)

Lynn Davies' winni
leap in the long jur
was among t
highlights of the Tok
Olympics, brough'
British viewers
radio link and satelli

Song and dance girl Millicent Martin presented her own series, **Mainly Millicent,** and was the Guild of Television Producers and Directors' Light Entertainment Personality of the Year. Patrick Wymark won the Best Actor award, and Rex Firkin the producer's award, for **The Plane Makers.** Popular American imports included **Burke's Law** and **The Beverly Hillbillies.** ITV initiated schools programmes for infants.

Lord Boothby was among those who discussed topical subjects in **After Dinner.** The series was recorded by concealed cameras to avoid inhibiting the conversation.

Andrew Faulds, later a Labour MP, starred in a crime series, **The Protectors,** Edwin Richfield in **It's Dark Outside,** and Alfie Bass and Bill Fraser in the comedy series, **Foreign Affairs.**

Eamonn Andrews joined ITV from the BBC on a three-year contract. His first assignment was as host to a variety of well-known guests in the pioneering programme **The Eamonn Andrews Show.**

1965

ITV celebrated the beginning of its second decade with a dinner at London's Guildhall, at which Prime Minister Harold Wilson said: "Independent television has become part of our national anatomy. More than that, it has become part of our social system and part of our national way of life."

Sir Winston Churchill, another British institution, died, and his majestic state funeral was watched by 350 million via Eurovision.

Edward Heath succeeded Sir Alec Douglas-Home as the new Tory leader. Cigarette commercials were banned on ITV as part of an anti-smoking campaign, which resulted in an £8 million-a-year loss of advertising revenue. The combined television and radio licence went up by £1 to £5.

The ITA began consultations with producers, writers and script editors about current output and to exchange ideas for the future.

ITV's documentary approach to the five-hour, live outside broadcast of Sir Winston Churchill's funeral included commentary by Brian Connell, narration by Sir Laurence Olivier, Joseph C. Harsch and Paul Scofield. An edited version, called **The Valiant Man,** was transmitted later.

1965

Redcap introduced a now-style detective: John Thaw as a tough sergeant in the Royal Military Police Special Investigation Branch, whose role was to fight crime in the Army. (ABC)

Front Page Story was made by Rex Firkin and Wilfred Greatorex, producer and script editor of **The Power Game.** This newspaper series had the underlying theme of the individual battling against his persecutors. (ATV)

John Wilder, the ruthless politician of the boardroom in **The Plane Makers,** came back to the screen in **The Power Game.** Now knighted and a merchant banker, he was again played by Patrick Wymark, with Barbara Murray as Lady Wilder. (ATV)

The intelligence agents played by Michael Aldridge and Richard Vernon used their intellectual powers to solve security problems in **The Man in Room 17.** (Granada)

111

The Successor, a **Play of the Week,** was about a conclave of cardinals choosing a new Pope. Rupert Davies—formerly TV's **Maigret**—beat the typecasting problem to play the Pope. (Anglia)

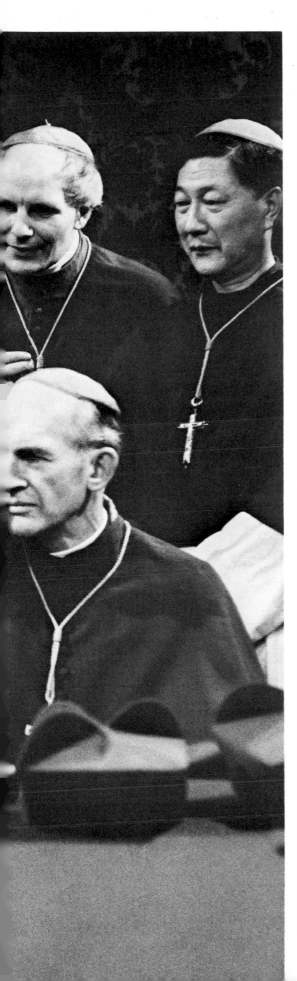

Two lusty Jacobean plays were presented under the title **Blood and Thunder**. Diana Rigg and Gene Anderson starred in Thomas Middleton's **Women Beware Women**. (Granada.)

Following the **Golden Hour** programmes of music and ballet came **Golden Drama**, a two-hour production from a London theatre, in which 30 actors presented dramatic excerpts. Included was Peter O'Toole with soliloquies from **Hamlet**. (ATV)

1965

Saturday afternoons became synonymous with sport when ITV launched **World of Sport,** introduced by Eamonn Andrews.

An international quartet of detectives fought criminals against a glamorous South of France background in **Riviera Police.** (Rediffusion)

Thunderbirds, a sophisticated puppet series about an international rescue organisation, was backed by a massive merchandising of toys and comics based on characters such as Lady Penelope and her chauffeur, Parker. (ATV)

Crime in war was the theme of the drama series **Court Martial.** In a bid for sales in the U.S., the two lawyer officers were Americans, played by Bradford Dillman and Peter Graves. (ATV)

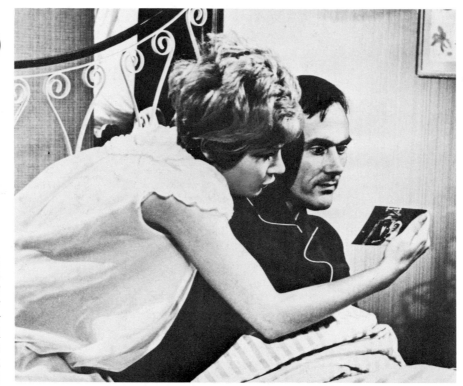

Blackmail – for money, power or love – was among the increasing number of anthology drama series. Dudley Foster and Ann Bell were the stars of this one, **First Offender.** (Rediffusion)

David Kossoff used his own words to tell children stories from the Old Testament in the Sunday series, **Storytime.** (ATV)

Public Eye explored new ground, introducing Alfred Burke as a believable private investigator who never used a gun or met big-time criminals. (ABC)

The Variety Club's ITV
personality of the year
was Bernard Braden,
who also won a
Television Society
silver medal for
On the Braden Beat.
The Variety Club's
showbusiness
personalities of the
year were Morecambe
and Wise, while
Jimmy Tarbuck was
voted the most
promising newcomer.
The Screen Writers'
Guild voted **The Plane
Makers** the best
television series.
The Queen's 10-day
State visit to West
Germany was brought
to the ITV screen live
via Eurovision.
Mr. Swindley, played
in **Coronation Street**
by Arthur Lowe,
achieved a series of
his own–as assistant
manager of a store in
Pardon the Expression.
Diana Rigg joined
The Avengers as the
widowed Emma Peel,
a replacement for
Honor Blackman's
Cathy Gale.
A new American
series was **Peyton Place**,
with Mia Farrow
and Ryan O'Neal.

1966

Continuing uncertainty about the future of British television, in particular the allocation of a fourth channel and the timing of the conversion from 405 lines to 625, caused the ITA to extend existing programme company contracts to 1968.

It then announced that the number of major companies would be increased from four to five in 1968. To make the division of the London area more equal, the weekend company would take over at 7.0 pm on Friday instead of on Saturday morning.

A General Election decided that Harold Wilson should stay at No. 10, and he had a dramatic but fruitless meeting on HMS Tiger with breakaway Rhodesia's leader, Ian Smith. England won the World Cup, beating West Germany 4–2.

A proposal that television cameras should be allowed experimentally into the House of Commons was defeated by one vote.

David Frost began a twice-weekly **Frost Programme**, in which he interviewed well-known people – from Mick Jagger to Frank Cousins. Audience contributions were "orchestrated"– Frost's description of the skilful way he stimulated the debate. (Rediffusion)

The drama series **Mrs. Thursday** starred Kathleen Harrison as a charlady who inherited a fortune. Creator Lord Ted Willis claimed that it took just 20 seconds to sell the idea to Lew (later Sir Lew) Grade. (ATV)

Intrigue examined the topical subject of industrial espionage, and starred Edward Judd as the counter-agent. (ABC)

Weavers Green was a twice-weekly look at life in a Norfolk village (Anglia)

Steve Forrest played a jet-age dealer in antiques in **The Baron,** a series based on a character created by John Creasey. (ATV)

1966

Victorian tales of the supernatural were dramatised in the series **Mystery and Imagination.** David Buck appeared as the linking central figure and is seen with Virginia McKenna in **The Phantom Lover.** (ABC)

Who Were the British?
set out to trace a
pedigree for ancient
Britons and was
Prof. Glyn Daniel's
contribution to the
popularisation of
archaeology on tele-
vision. (Anglia)

Presenting a new
breed of anti-hero,
The Informer was a
disbarred barrister
earning a rich
living as a tipster
for police and
insurance companies.
Ian Hendry starred
in the title role,
with Heather Sears
as his wife, and Jean
Marsh his mistress.
(Rediffusion)

A thriller series for children, **Orlando** followed the daring adventures of a smuggler, played by Sam Kydd, who had first appeared in the adult series, **Crane.** (Rediffusion)

George and the Dragon starred the new situation comedy team of Sidney James and Peggy Mount, who played handyman and housekeeper in a stately home. (ATV)

All Square explored Michael Bentine's inimitable brand of comedy. This zany series found humour in everything from duelling to the esoteric sport of dwile-flonking. (ATV)

The Stories of D.H. Lawrence, mainly about Nottinghamshire mining villages, were adapted into a drama series that kept faithfully to the spirit of the original. (Granada)

Terence Rattigan's **Nelson – A Study in Miniature,** with Michael Bryant as the Admiral, was written at the suggestion of Prince Philip, who later introduced the play on screen. (ATV)

England, led by Bobby Moore, achieved a memorable victory in The World Cup. ITV's nightly coverage of games throughout England was presented by Eamonn Andrews.

Alastair Burnet introduced ITN's second General Election programme in 11 months, and won the Guild of Television Producers and Directors' Richard Dimbleby award. Geoffrey Cox, Editor of ITN, was knighted. The Variety Club of Great Britain made a special double award to Hughie Green, of **Double Your Money,** and **Take Your Pick's** Michael Miles for the continuing popularity of their programmes. Green took his **Double Your Money** team to Russia to stage a programme with Muscovite contestants.

Danger Man, starring Patrick McGoohan, won a Hollywood Screen Producers' Guild award for the best-produced TV programme.

A craze for **Batman,** the pre-war strip cartoon for children, brought an American television series, with Adam West as the caped crusader. Documentary producer Adrian Cowell and cameraman Chris Menges returned from their travels in Thailand, Tibet, Laos and Burma with two highly praised programmes, **Light of Asia** and **The Opium Trail.**

1967

The ITA invited franchise applications for the new contract period beginning in 1968, and many strangely named consortia were formed to bid for them. There was a total of 36 applications from 16 new groups and the 14 existing companies.

ITA Chairman Lord Hill announced the successful organisations in June, after which Prime Minister Wilson–in a surprise and controversial decision–moved him to the Chairmanship of the BBC.

BBC2 was allowed to go into colour on 625 lines UHF; ITV was also making programmes in colour but they were shown in black and white. The colour was seen only in America and other countries to which the programmes were sold.

ITN launched **News at Ten,** the first regular half-hour news on a major channel. Within days it was an established success after showing exciting film of Col. Colin Mitchell leading his Highlanders in the re-taking of the Crater district of Aden.

Israel mauled the Arabs in the Six Day War and the revolutionary Che Guevara was killed in Bolivia. Dr. Christian Barnard performed his first heart transplant. Jeremy Thorpe succeeded Jo Grimond as Liberal leader, and the BBC introduced a pop radio channel and the first local radio.

News at Ten combined news and analysis in a programme twice the length of the bulletin it replaced. The new format introduced a two-man newscaster system enabling late items to be fed to the man off-camera. (ITN)

1967

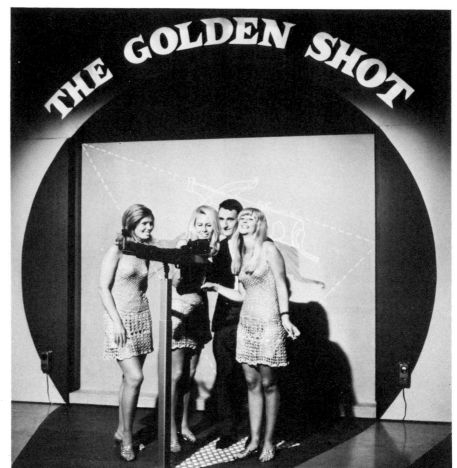

THE GOLDEN SHOT

The Golden Shot was a new type of TV game in which the contestants fired bolts from an electronic bow at novelty targets. Jackie Rae was first compere. (ATV)

At Last the 1948 Show set a new trend, with John Cleese, Tim Brooke-Taylor and Graham Chapman exploring the type of lunatic comedy that would lead to **Monty Python's Flying Circus** and **The Goodies**. It also starred lovely Aimi Macdonald in a dumb blonde role. (Rediffusion)

Television created a new sport in rallycross. Devised specially for **World of Sport** by director Robert Reid, it featured saloon cars in events combining road and rough country racing. (ABC)

Adapted from three novels by Phyllis Bentley, **Inheritance** related the saga of a Yorkshire mill family from 1812 to 1965. The main actors played several generations of the Oldroyd family. (Granada)

Ronnie Corbett portrayed a dithery, tongue-tied little man in a comedy series about life in suburbia, **No, That's Me Over Here**. (Rediffusion)

Richard Bradford was McGill in **Man In a Suitcase**. A bounty hunter, always on the move, he typified the rugged hero of the Sixties. (ATV)

Callan, a series developed from a play about a licensed-to-kill British agent, created a hero to rank among TV's all-time greats. It made Edward Woodward one of Britain's most popular actors, and eventually won a Writers' Guild award for creator James Mitchell. (ABC)

Featured in **The Odd Man** and **It's Dark Outside,** Chief Insp. Rose (William Mervyn) won his own series, **Mr. Rose,** in which he had retired to write his memoirs. (Granada)

One of the most extensive open air sets ever built for a TV drama was constructed at Elstree for **Market in Honey Lane,** a series about a London street market, its stallholders and customers. (ATV)

The Prisoner was an imaginative series concerning the mind-bending, will-sapping treatment meted out to a former British agent. Patrick McGoohan was deviser, producer and star and also wrote, directed and edited some of the episodes. (ATV)

Acclaimed many times as a new star, Des O'Connor finally proved his potential as a dollar earner when **The Des O'Connor Show** was exported to America. (ATV)

Tonight with Dave Allen was described as a "late night miscellany". The Irish comedian conducted interviews and risked his neck in many strange stunts. (ATV)

1967

More than 20 million viewers watched the marriage of Elsie Tanner and Steve Tanner in **Coronation Street,** Britain's top serial. (Granada)

Pudgy comedian Joe Baker so impressed an ATV staff party at which he performed that he was given his own TV series, **My Man Joe.** (ATV)

John Bluthal a
Joe Lynch starrec
Never Mind
Quality, Feel
Width, a come
series about an Iri
Jewish tailor
partnership.(Al

Prince Philip introduced **The Enchanted Isles**, a programme about the wildlife of the Galapagos in the Pacific. It won awards in Monte Carlo and America. Comedy actors given series during the year included Arthur Lowe, (**Turn Out the Lights**); Harry H. Corbett, (**Mr. Aitch**); and Joe Baker (**My Man Joe**). Children's series included **The Lion, the Witch and the Wardrobe**, the C. S. Lewis allegory, **The Flower of Gloster**, about children on a narrow boat traversing canals from North Wales to London; and **Sexton Blake**, the adventures of the enduring detective.

1968

The new ITV companies began operating in July. Among them were Yorkshire, whose founders included Alan Whicker, London Weekend (David Frost), Harlech (Richard Burton) and Thames, which was a merger of ABC and Rediffusion.

Simultaneously, a new TVTimes with regional editions was launched to replace separate programme journals. Favourite programmes, such as **Double Your Money** and **Take Your Pick,** were discontinued and new ones introduced in sweeping changes. The BBC competed strenuously for the mass audience by scheduling new series of popular programmes at peak times on its major channel.

Russian tanks invaded Czechoslovakia to smash Alexander Dubcek's liberalising regime. Pictures of students shouting defiance at the Russians were transmitted live by Czech television before it was shut down, and relayed via Eurovision.

Elsewhere in a violent year, Martin Luther King and Robert Kennedy were assassinated and there were civil rights demonstrations in Londonderry. Richard Nixon became America's President.

While educationists argued the merits of comprehensive and grammar schools, **Please Sir!** won laughs with the story of a recently qualified teacher in a tough secondary school. As the harassed master, John Alderton won the Royal Television Society's award for "outstanding male personality". (LWT)

We Have Ways of Making You Laugh was the challenging title Frank Muir chose for one of the first programmes resulting from his appointment as head of light entertainment with one of the new companies. He also starred in the show. (LWT)

One of many ideas from Lord Ted Willis, **Virgin of the Secret Service** was a spoof spy series concerning an early secret agent, Capt. Robert Virgin, who travelled the Empire in the early 1900s. (ATV)

Black Power salutes
at the Mexico
Olympic Games,
which were televised
live via satellite
and Eurovision.

Vince Powell and Harry Driver created some of the most popular comedy series of the Sixties. **Nearest and Dearest** teamed Hylda Baker and Jimmy Jewel as a brother and sister who inherited a run-down pickle business. (Granada)

Children were given an insight into the period of World War One through **Tom Grattan's War,** the story of a boy living in that era. (Yorkshire)

Frontier looked at the theme of British Imperial history – little explored at this time – for a drama series about soldiers on the North West Frontier of India. (Thames)

1968

Established by **The Power Game** as one of Britain's top TV actors, Patrick Wymark was invited to choose four **Playhouse** productions in which he would like to star. Among his choices was August Strindberg's **The Father.** (ATV)

Do Not Adjust Your Set was a trend-setting series for children which won a Prix Jeunesse first prize at Munich. (Rediffusion)

A new-style TVTimes, reflecting the changed image of ITV, was introduced in September. Its 13 regional editions replaced existing ITV programme journals produced by a number of publishers.

Patrick Cargill was the endearing head of the Glover family in **Father, Dear Father**, the story of a divorcee's bid to rear two nubile daughters. (Thames)

A master criminal's bid for world domination was the exciting theme of **Freewheelers,** a series aimed at teenagers. (Southern)

A Man Of Our Times was a dramatic examination of the prototypal modern man and his ambitions and fears. The role was played by George Cole. (Rediffusion)

Horrifying film from Nigeria showed the execution of an officer for his part in the murder of Biafrans. (ITN)

Linda Thorson
succeeded Diana
Rigg as Patrick
Macnee's partner in
The Avengers.
Nemone Lethbridge
wrote **The Franchise
Trail,** a play that
satirised the rush
for ITV contracts.
David Frost introduced
everything from
interviews to variety
in his three weekly
programmes. Two of
his "confrontations"
with subjects who
were later arrested
led to an outcry about
"trial by television."
The video disc was
used to provide
instant replays
in sporting events.
A £5 supplementary
licence for colour TV
was introduced; a
colour licence cost £10.

1969

The year of colour for ITV and BBC1. Lord Aylestone –who succeeded Lord Hill as chairman of the ITA – performed ITV's switch-on ceremony.

Otherwise, it was a year of consolidation as ITV overcame the difficulties that had followed its reconstruction. The collapse of the Emley Moor transmitter mast in Yorkshire did not help, but ITV re-established itself in the ratings as the most popular channel.

And on one of the most memorable nights in history, the night when man landed on the Moon, professional critics and viewers agreed that ITV's 15-hour presentation was superior to that of the BBC.

The cost of television licences rose by £1–to £6 for black and white sets and £11 for colour. But the number of colour sets increased from 100,000 to 270,000.

President de Gaulle resigned. Prime Minister Wilson sent an invasion force to the island of Anguilla, where a self-appointed President was demanding independence. The voting age was reduced from 21 to 18, and the Open University was founded.

Man On the Moon was ITV's longest-ever production–from 6.0pm on July 20 to 9.0 the following morning. News and comment on the Moon mission alternated with David Frost's gala variety show and phone-in session. Alastair Burnet headed ITN's team in the "Moon studio", with comment from TVTimes Science Editor Peter Fairley.

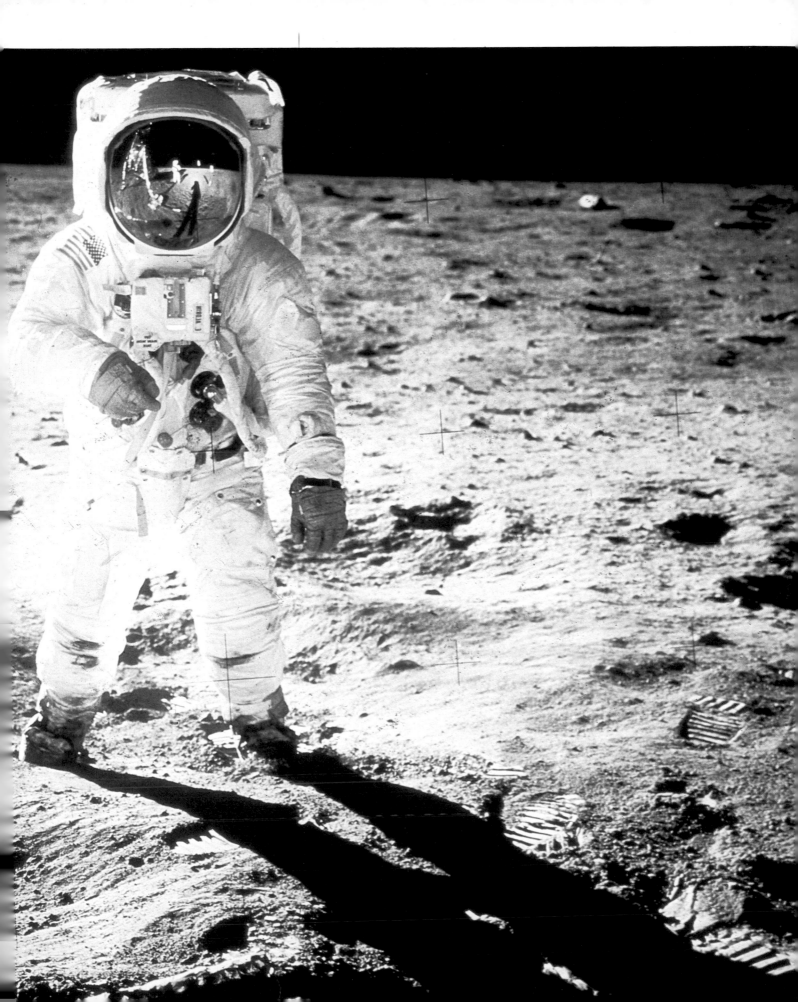

The Dustbinmen, Jack Rosenthal's comedy series about the crew of a dustcart known as Thunderbird Three, achieved the unusual distinction of reaching No. One in the JICTAR ratings with each of its six episodes. (Granada)

Three of the most talented producers and directors of the BBC's **Wednesday Play** series – Tony Garnett, Kenith Trodd and James McTaggart – formed their own company, Kestrel Productions, to make plays for ITV. One of the most successful was **Bangelstein's Boys,** the story of a rugby club's weekend excursion. (LWT)

Continuing the role he had created in **Gazette**, Gerald Harper starred as **Hadleigh,** the smooth Yorkshire landowner who was to become one of the most popular characters on ITV. (Yorkshire)

The Mind of Mr. J. G. Reeder starred Hugh Burden as Edgar Wallace's mild-mannered detective with an intuitive understanding of the criminal's devious intellect. (Thames)

151

Stars on Sunday was the first religious series to enter the Top 20 viewing figures. This was achieved by mixing actors and pop stars, prelates and politicians in lavish settings, to sing, or read verses from the Bible. (Yorkshire)

Doctor in the House was another comedy series which was to receive popular acclaim. Based on Richard Gordon's novels about young medical men, it developed its theme through 138 episodes and over more than five years. (LWT)

The comedy series **On the Buses** made its debut, with Reg Varney as the genial bus driver. A year later, Sun readers were to vote it their "top series". (LWT)

The Gold Robbers was a skilfully made drama series about the detective work carried out by a dedicated policeman (played by Peter Vaughan), following a massive bullion theft. (LWT)

1969

Instead of writing a book, Lord Louis Mountbatten chose to present his memoirs on ITV. **The Life and Times of Lord Mountbatten,** filmed around the world, won Producer Peter Morley a Royal Television Society silver medal. An S.F.T.A. award for best script went to historian John Terraine. (Thames)

Rodney Bewes was co-writer, co-producer and star of **Dear Mother ...Love Albert.** This comedy series hinged on the lively letters a young man sent home to his mother (Thames)

Special Branch saw the debut of a new-style police investigator. Derren Nesbitt played Det.-Chief Insp. Jordan as a fashionable dresser, with floral shirts, wide ties and flared trousers. (Thames)

1969

A new character to replace John Wilder, the ruthless businessman played by Patrick Wymark in **The Power Game,** arrived with the creation of David Main in **The Main Chance.** John Stride starred as the tough, ambitious young solicitor. (Yorkshire)

Eamonn Andrews revived his biographical show, **This is Your Life,** which he had presented on BBC Television from 1953 to 1964. Andrews' faith was justified and it was soon the most popular show in Britain. (Thames)

The Investiture of Prince Charles as Prince of Wales was a day of pageantry at Caernarvon Castle. ITV's commentators were Brian Connell and Wynford Vaughan-Thomas, and the stirring tribute to Wales was read by actor Richard Burton.

A gambling innovation was the introduction of **The ITV Seven.** Viewers placed accumulator bets covering seven races from two meetings shown in **World of Sport.** The advantage was that punters were eligible for a proportion of their winnings even if only five or six consecutive selections won.

ITN set out to discover the truth about Loch Ness Monster stories and mounted a big expedition involving a midget submarine and echo sounders. But the Monster failed to appear before the waiting cameras.

Ronnie Barker, who appeared as a doddering peer named Lord Rustless in **Hark at Barker,** was the Variety Club's choice as ITV Personality of the Year. But TVTimes readers voted Tom Jones top of their poll.

Male of the Species, a trilogy of plays by Alun Owen, was introduced by Laurence Olivier and starred Sean Connery, Michael Caine and Paul Scofield. An unknown, Anna Calder-Marshall, who co-starred in all three, won an Emmy award.

Royal Family, the most human look yet at the Queen and her family, was a 115-minute documentary made by a joint BBC/ITV consortium.

1970

Sir Robert Fraser, Director General of the ITA since its inception, and chief architect of ITV's federal structure, retired at the age of 66. He said that the most significant development of the past 15 years had been "the growth of TV as a medium of information alongside TV as a medium of entertainment, which it was – almost pure and simple – in 1955. Now it is theatre and newspaper in one – a pregnant social change."

The events of the year, in which Edward Heath became Premier, underlined Sir Robert's words. On Budget Day, there was an explosion on board Apollo 13 as it journeyed towards the Moon. Alastair Burnet – ITV's man for big occasions – fronted a combined Budget and Apollo programme that continued until 4am when the astronauts were out of danger.

And ITN gained a world scoop with exclusive film of the blowing up by Palestinian guerillas of three airliners they had hijacked to Jordan.

But ITV's profits dropped to their lowest level for a decade, due largely to the increased costs of colour transmissions and the fact that the companies charged no premium for commercials in colour.

The longest, costliest ITV drama series to date was **A Family at War.** Created by John Finch, it told the story of a Liverpool family at war within itself and was set in the framework of World War Two. (Granada)

158

Manhunt, a serial about a French Resistance girl and an RAF pilot on the run through occupied France, featured Alfred Lynch, Peter Barkworth and beautiful discovery Cyd Hayman. (LWT)

Phyllis Calvert, former star of British films, became a star of television as **Kate**, a magazine columnist answering readers' personal problems. (Yorkshire)

The expert and forthright views of ITV's World Cup panel – Bob McNab, Pat Crerand, Derek Dougan and Malcolm Allison, encouraged by presenters Jimmy Hill and Brian Moore – rivalled the football itself. England were eliminated in the quarter finals.

161

The Lovers, a comedy series about an attractive but ingenuous courting couple – played by Paula Wilcox and Richard Beckinsale – won a Writers' Guild award for Geoffrey Lancashire and Jack Rosenthal. (Granada)

Crime of Passion, a series of fictional murder trials set in a French court, was the creation of Lord Ted Willis. (ATV)

Romance among old age pensioners sounded an unpromising subject for comedy, but Irene Handl and Wilfred Pickles gave **For the Love of Ada** wide appeal. (Thames)

Adrian Cowell, an
independent
producer specialising
in programmes from
remote places, went
to the Amazon jungle
of Brazil to make
**The Tribe That Hides
From Man,** which won
a Prix Italia award,
and a silver medal
at the Venice
Film Festival. (ATV)

Humphrey Burton
edited and presented
Aquarius, a major
new arts programme
which was shown
at first fortnightly,
later weekly. (LWT)

Simon Dee, once a disc jockey on a pirate radio ship, became host of an entertaining new chat show. The series was ended after he quarrelled with executives over choice of guests. (LWT)

Alan Whicker roved the world interviewing a rich variety of subjects—ranging from Francois (Papa Doc) Duvalier, the dictator of Haiti, to the Bluebell dancers of Paris. (Yorkshire)

One of the answers to a plea from the ITA for more imaginative series for children was **Catweazle,** in which an 11th century magician found himself transported to modern England. (LWT)

Charlie Nairn and his television team lived for five weeks among South American Indians to film **A Clearing in the Jungle** for an occasional series, **The Disappearing World.** (Granada)

Because all scheduled flights in and out of Jordan had been cancelled, ITN chartered a 120-seat airliner to fly out exclusive film of the destruction of hijacked jets on Dawson's Field. (ITN)

In the six-part documentary series **The Day Before Yesterday,** producer Phillip Whitehead – later to become a Labour MP – examined the period 1945 to 1963 with the help of people who shaped the history of those years.

Ronald Fraser starred as Badger in **The Misfit,** the comic misadventures of an Englishman who returned from the Colonies to a vastly changed Britain. The series won Roy Clarke a Writers' Guild award.

Coronation Street reached its 1,000th episode and received the Sun newspaper's "top series" award.

Singer/actor Tommy Steele was one of the stars in ITV's lively production of **Twelfth Night**.

1971

Chancellor of the Exchequer Anthony Barber eased the credit squeeze in a July mini-Budget and the hire purchase of colour television sets rocketed. Manufacturers could not meet the demand and had to ration supplies to shops, where prices were now displayed in decimal currency.

Within a year, a million new colour sets had been licensed, in spite of a £1 increase in licence fees – to £7 for black and white and £12 for colour.

A £10 million reduction in the levy on ITV's advertising income also encouraged the television industry. Some other concerns had a less cheerful year: Rolls-Royce and Upper Clyde Shipbuilders went into liquidation and the Daily Sketch ceased publication.

There were troubles at London Weekend Television, where financial problems had hindered the company from fulfilling its original programme plans, and a number of key executives resigned.

The troubles ended after newspaper owner Rupert Murdoch took a financial stake in the company and John Freeman, former British Ambassador to the U.S., and a noted television broadcaster, was appointed chairman and chief executive.

A saga that was to run for five years and 68 episodes, **Upstairs, Downstairs** began the dramatic story of the Bellamy family and their servants in the Edwardian era. The programme was voted Best Drama Series by the Society of Film and Television Arts. (LWT)

Former pop singer Adam Faith emerged as an actor of charm in **Budgie**, the story of an unsuccessful crook in seedy Soho. (LWT)

A television team accompanied Chris Bonington on his successful assault on the previously unscaled South Face of Annapurna in the Himalayas for **The Hardest Way Up.** (Thames)

Moving on from the politics, diplomacy and money of **The Power Game,** Wilfred Greatorex created **Hine,** about the manoeuvring and money of an international arms dealer, played by Barrie Ingham. (ATV)

Persuasion was an elegant, five-part series based on Jane Austen's posthumously published novel about lost love reborn. (Granada)

The unusual casting of American Richard Chamberlain –formerly television's Dr. Kildare – as **Hamlet** attracted a wide audience for this two-hour Shakespearian production. (ATV)

After three years on BBC Television in **Not In Front of the Children,** Wendy Craig moved to ITV to play a similarly scatterbrained role, appearing as a widow with two children in **...And Mother Makes Three.** (Thames)

America's Tony Curtis and Britain's Roger Moore were teamed in **The Persuaders,** a slick action series and one of the shows that helped ATV win a third Queen's Award to Industry for overseas sales. (ATV)

1971

The Comedians used six or eight stand-up comics per show and edited their gags into a succession of non-stop laughs. The programme's new approach made stars of little known comedians. (Granada)

With the teaming of stars as important as the storyline in situation comedy, **Bless This House** created a winning combination –Sidney James and Diana Coupland as husband and wife, with Sally Geeson and Robin Stewart as their children. (Thames)

The Fenn Street Gang, sequel to **Please Sir!** traced the adventures of Form 5C's pupils in post-school life. (LWT)

1971

Prince Philip launched a wildlife preservation campaign when he introduced film from Kenya in **Now or Never**, in the **Survival** series. (Anglia)

Lord Snowdon directed his third film, **Born to be Small**, a compassionate documentary about "people of restricted growth". (ATV)

Man at the Top was a series reflecting the permissiveness of the time through the amorous exploits of John Braine's hero, Joe Lampton (played by Kenneth Haigh). (Thames)

ITN celebrated 1,000 editions of **News at Ten,** of which 632 had featured in the Top Twenty.

Prince Andrew and Prince Edward appeared with the Queen in her Christmas Day television broadcast.

The campaign for equal opportunities for women received support from **Justice,** in which Margaret Lockwood played Harriet Peterson, a tough – but attractive – barrister, more than a match for male competition.

A political thriller series, **The Guardians** presented a chilling picture of a Britain in which democracy had been replaced by quasi-military rule.

1972

Restrictions on television hours were swept away by the Government following a long campaign by ITV for more time. Christopher Chataway, the former ITN newscaster, made the announcement as Minister of Posts and Telecommunications. ITV immediately planned up to 20 extra hours of weekday television to provide a total of 105 hours viewing a week. The television day stretched to 15 hours and breakfast time programmes were forecast. In the meantime, new afternoon serials aimed chiefly at women were introduced and ITN added a lunchtime news bulletin. Television news covered many big stories during the year. Thirteen were shot dead in Londonderry when troops ended an illegal march. Arab guerillas murdered two members of the Israeli team in the Olympic village in Munich; later, nine hostages were killed when the terrorists were ambushed.

A state of emergency followed a strike by miners and brought severe restrictions on the use of electricity. The ITA became the Independent Broadcasting Authority (IBA) when it also assumed responsibility for proposed independent radio stations.

Country Matters, based on short stories by H. E. Bates and A. E. Coppard, brought new stature to the anthology drama series; the Society of Film and Television Arts voted it "Best Drama Series". (Granada)

Viennese waltzes played by the London Symphony Orchestra added an extra dimension to **The Strauss Family,** eight plays celebrating the 19th century composers. (ATV)

The endless search for new television detectives led to **Van der Valk,** with Barry Foster as the Amsterdam policeman of Nicholas Freeling's books. (Thames)

My Good Woman, an elegant comedy series set in the stockbroker belt, teamed Sylvia Syms, as a charity worker, and Leslie Crowther as her long-suffering husband. (ATV)

1972

Black Beauty, Anna Sewell's classic story for children about a girl and her horse, provided the basis for a drama series. (LWT)

Capitalising on the popularity of impressionists, **Who Do You Do?** featured the best-known in a series of fast-moving, half-hour shows. (LWT)

Sale of the Century, a new quiz show, offered successful contestants the opportunity to acquire expensive products at special bargain prices. (Anglia)

The camp humour of Larry Grayson made him the comic of the year and **Shut That Door!** – the title of his series – a popular catchphrase. (ATV)

Love Thy Neighbour tackled the controversial subject of race relations with shrewd but unbiased good humour. It derived its laughs from the relationship between black and white couples. (Thames)

1972

The 24-part **Arthur of the Britons,** with Oliver Tobias playing him as a tribal warlord, was claimed to be the biggest production undertaken by one of ITV's smaller companies. (HTV)

To avoid irritating viewers with duplicate coverage, ITV left live transmission of the Munich Olympics to the BBC and included nightly highlights in news bulletins.

Adam Smith was ITV's first religious drama series made for Sunday evening viewing, and was about a minister in a Scottish country town. (Granada)

Robert Kee presented **First Report,** the new lunchtime news, with a greater degree of freedom than had ever been given to a newscaster. (ITN)

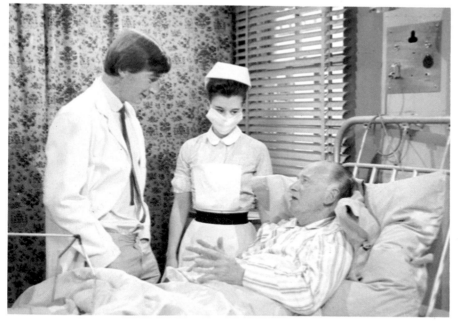

All those viewers – and television executives – who had regretted the ending of **Emergency-Ward 10** in 1967, now welcomed a new serial, **General Hospital,** for afternoon viewing. (ATV)

Another new afternoon serial, made possible by the de-restriction of television hours, was **Emmerdale Farm,** a twice-weekly story about a farming family in the dales. (Yorkshire)

A row broke out when the IBA suggested that a Glyndebourne production of Verdi's opera **Macbeth** should be screened at Christmas; viewers protested that they wanted lighter fare. In the event, the opera was shown on December 27 and was watched by two million – enough to have filled Covent Garden Opera House daily for two years. MP's again barred television cameras from the House of Commons, this time by 26 votes.

Weekend World, a Sunday newspaper of the screen introduced by Peter Jay, made its debut; it was highly praised, although the audience available at 11am on Sundays was small. The programme was subsequently transmitted at 11.30am, then became a regular midday show.

1973

Viewers acclaimed **The World at War,** a massive 26-week production about World War Two, while a ceasefire prevailed in Vietnam. But letter and fire bombs exploded in London, British frigates fended off gunboats in a battle over Iceland's disputed 50-mile fishing limits, and trade unions defied the rulings of the Industrial Relations Court.

Echoes of wartime were evoked by the issue of petrol coupons to motorists in a fuel crisis that followed the raising of oil prices by Middle East producers.

The wedding of the year was that of Princess Anne and Capt. Mark Phillips, who gave television interviews two days before their marriage. The most colourful legal battle of the year concerned **Warhol,** an ITV programme against which Ross McWhirter obtained an injunction on the grounds it constituted an offence against good taste. This was later lifted by the Court of Appeal, which ruled that censorship of ITV programmes was the IBA's job.

A 50-strong team spent nearly four years preparing **The World at War.** A meticulously researched history of World War Two, it won an Emmy award for outstanding documentary treatment. (Thames)

Laurence Olivier – narrator of **The World at War** – won an Emmy award for his performance in Eugene O'Neill's tragic play, **Long Day's Journey Into Night,** performed by the original National Theatre cast. (ATV)

Shabby Tiger was a seven-part adaptation of a Howard Spring novel about a wild Irish girl and her love for an artist. (Granada)

ITV kept pace with developments on the pop music scene with **James Paul McCartney,** in which the ex-Beatle introduced his new group, Wings. (ATV)

It is comparatively rare for a TV series to be built around a woman, but this happened with **Beryl's Lot,** the story of a middle aged char, played by Carmel McSharry. (Yorkshire)

An ITV team went behind the Iron Curtain to film **Olga,** a profile of the 17-year-old Russian gymnast Olga Korbut, whose grace and charm won hearts at the 1972 Olympics. (Granada)

1973

ITV devoted nearly six hours to the wedding of Princess Anne and Capt. Mark Phillips. Twenty-eight camera crews and eight commentators covered the glittering occasion, with Andrew Gardner describing the scene live in Westminster Abbey.

Richard Burton and Elizabeth Taylor – members of the consortium that set up HTV in 1967 – starred in **Divorce His: Divorce Hers,** a two-part drama screened before their marriage hit trouble. (HTV)

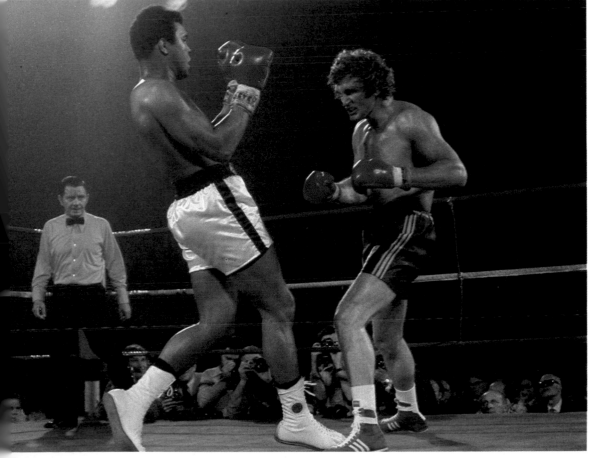

The fight of the year and exclusive to ITV – European Heavyweight Champion Joe Bugner was beaten on points over 12 rounds by Muhammad Ali in Las Vegas. (Independent Television Sport Production)

1973

The **Bröntes of Haworth** was a dramatic evocation of the lives of the remarkable, novel-writing Brönte sisters – Anne, Emily and Charlotte – and their family. (Yorkshire)

Russell Harty was host of a controversial chat show and won a Pye award as Outstanding New Male TV Personality. Alan Browning, Pat Phoenix and David Bailey joined him on this occasion. (LWT)

In **The Stanley Baxter Big Picture Show,** Baxter's superbly accurate impersonations were superimposed on spectacular settings. He won the S.F.T.A. award for Best Light Entertainment Programme. (LWT)

A new element was brought to television sport with **Indoor League.** Introduced by former England fast bowler Fred Trueman, it featured darts, table skittles, shove ha'penny and American pool. (Yorkshire)

Sam, a new work by John Finch, creator of **A Family at War,** concerned a boy growing up in the impoverished Thirties and was an immediate success. (Granada)

The Death of Adolf Hitler, one of many plays and films in 1973 about the Fuehrer, gave Frank Finlay the opportunity for a memorably ranting performance. (LWT)

Jonathan Dimbleby's **This Week** report from Ethiopia led to £1,500,000 being raised in Britain for famine relief, and won him an award named after his father, Richard Dimbleby. (Thames)

Helen – A Woma Today was a natu successor to **A M Of Our Tim** Helen was played Alison Fiske in a se that commented contemporary mo and marriage. (LV

ORACLE, the IBA's system for printing out the latest news and other information on a domestic TV set, was demonstrated for the first time.

London Broadcasting, Britain's first independent radio station, went on the air on October 8. It was followed by Capital on October 16, and Radio Clyde at the end of the year.

Kung Fu became a craze with the showing in some regions of the Hollywood series starring David Carradine as the inscrutable, high-kicking monk, Caine.

Veteran comic Jimmy Jewel turned actor for **Spring and Autumn**, a poignant comedy series about the relationship between young and old.

Hunter's Walk, a police series set in the East Midlands, achieved a high degree of realism by concentrating mainly on the solving of small time crime.

Meanwhile, a new series of **Special Branch** introduced new detectives, played by George Sewell and Patrick Mower, and was filmed on location.

Transmission of **Warhol**, the David Bailey documentary about the pop artist Andy Warhol, was delayed by a court action. But it was eventually shown to a large audience, most of whom found it boring rather than offensive, according to an IBA survey.

197

1974

The television year began with a 10.30pm curfew, which was imposed by the Government – along with a three-day working week – following industrial action by miners, power engineers and train drivers. The curfew ended after a General Election in February. Although this produced no overall majority in Parliament, Edward Heath yielded No. 10 to Harold Wilson and, in a November election, Labour won an overall majority.

The setting up by the new Government of the Committee on the Future of Broadcasting, under Lord Annan, left television's long-term future unpredictable. However, the immediate life of the ITV companies (due for a review of contracts in 1976) was extended by a further three years.

When Turkish paratroopers invaded Cyprus, ITN's Michael Nicholson gained a world scoop by being on the spot to interview them. Princess Anne escaped a kidnap attempt. President Nixon resigned in the aftermath of the Watergate scandal.

Churchill Centenary Year was marked by a distinguished drama series in which Lee Remick played the dazzling **Jennie, Lady Randolph Churchill.** (Thames)

1974

The Royal Shakespeare Company's two-and-a half-hour production of **Antony and Cleopatra,** with Richard Johnson and Janet Suzman, was voted Best Play of the Year by the Society of Film and Television Arts.

Intimate Strangers was another dramatic examination of middle class marriage and morality from Richard Bates, producer of **A Man Of Our Times** and **Helen – A Woman of Today.** (LWT)

My Old Man featured Clive Dunn (born Jan. 9, 1922) in the type of role which made him popular. (Yorkshire)

Dick Clement and
Ian La Frenais were
the most acclaimed
comedy scriptwriters
of the year. In their
Thick as Thieves,
Bob Hoskins was a
released prisoner
who found his wife
(Pat Ashton) sharing
the home with
his friend, played
by John Thaw. (LWT)

The Inheritors, a
drama series on the
topical theme of an
ancient family estate
being broken-up,
starred Peter Egan
and Robert
Urquhart (HTV)

1974

In **Napoleon and Love,** a major historical drama series by Philip Mackie, Ian Holm played the Emperor and Billie Whitelaw was Josephine. (Thames)

202

Set in the 19th century, **Boy Dominic** – a "family serial" for Sunday afternoons – followed the adventures of a 12-year-old seeking his shipwrecked father. (Yorkshire)

Kenneth More justified his surprise casting as G.K. Chesterton's **Father Brown**. Angela Douglas (Mrs. More) also appeared in the series. (ATV)

203

1974

Norman Wisdom returned for his second ITV comedy series, **A Little Bit of Wisdom**. (ATV)

John Mills and Lilli Palmer were among the international stars in **The Zoo Gang,** Paul Gallico's stories about French Resistance workers after the war. (ATV)

South Riding, based on Winifred Holtby's 1936 novel, was voted the Society of Film and Television Arts' Best Drama Series. Dorothy Tutin starred. (Yorkshire)

Sunley's Daughter traced the hardships endured by Joe Sunley and his daughter on their Yorkshire Moors farm, where they bred the much sought after Cleveland Bay horses. (Yorkshire)

A new scriptwriting team was acclaimed when playwrights Julia Jones and Donald Churchill joined forces to create **Moody and Pegg,** with Judy Cornwell and Derek Waring in the title roles. (Thames)

1974

Richard Beckinsale as student lodger, Leonard Rossiter as grasping landlord, in the comedy series **Rising Damp**. (Yorkshire)

The contemporary popularity of working men's clubs was reflected by one specially created for television, **Wheeltappers and Shunters Social Club**. (Granada)

Following **The Julie Andrews Hour**, a series which won seven Emmy Awards and the Silver Rose of Montreux in 1973, she starred in five one-hour spectaculars, including **Julie on Sesame Street**. (ATV)

For ITN's General Election coverage, a machine used for planning knitting patterns was coupled to the programme's computer. It printed out results and forecasts in instant diagrams.

"Open access" programmes, providing television time for organisations and pressure groups to present their views, were introduced in many regions.

The Prison, screened as the first **Armchair Cinema** presentation, was among Britain's earliest 90-minute, made-for-television films.

Peter Jay, of **Weekend World,** was the Royal Television Society's Personality of the Year. John Pilger introduced his own current affairs series during **Weekend World's** summer break.

Video cassette recorders became available for home use. Prized status symbols, at more than £400 they were £100 dearer than a colour set.

The House of Commons again barred television cameras – this time by 25 votes.

1975

It was **Edward the Seventh**'s year. This distinguished 13-part series was a glorious success; in part, perhaps, because of the contrast between its elegant portrayal of a bygone era and the violence of 1975.

South Vietnam fell to the Vietcong, Irish bombs exploded in London's West End, and 41 people died in London Underground's worst crash. Dissension about the Common Market led to Britain's first national referendum. There was rampaging inflation, and television licences were among the items that became dearer – £18 for colour and £8 for black and white. Meanwhile, ITV companies, which do not benefit from licence revenue, complained about rising costs.

Mrs. Thatcher became leader of the Conservative party and Lady Plowden Chairman of the IBA. With Sir Michael Swann already at the BBC, both networks were now headed by educationists.

Proceedings in the Commons were broadcast live by radio in a month-long experiment, but television cameras were again barred, by 12 votes.

Timothy West was crowned **Edward the Seventh** in a series that won critical acclaim, topped the ratings and was voted Best Drama Series of 1975 by the British Academy of Film and Television Arts. (ATV)

1975

Celebrity Squares, an Anglicised version of a top American quiz show in which contestants decided whether guest celebrities had answered questions correctly. (ATV)

My Brother's Keeper took a humorous look at the controversial subject of law and order, with George Layton as a policeman, Jonathan Lynn as his wastrel twin. (Granada)

Joy Adamson's story of how she reared the lioness Elsa – subject of two British films – was the basis for **Born Free**, an American series filmed in Kenya.

Adapted from A. J. Cronin's best-selling novel of the Thirties, **The Stars Look Down** was the story of a north eastern mining community during the early years of this century. (Granada)

The Sweeney, a filmed crime series, set new standards for realistic fights, dramatic car chases and crackling dialogue. John Thaw starred as Det.-Insp. Jack Regan. (Thames)

Nutritionist Dr. Magnus Pyke (65), became an unlikely TV star as a resident expert in the popular science show, **Don't Ask Me,** which was regularly in the Top Twenty. (Yorkshire)

A bold documentary venture, **The Naked Civil Servant** was the dramatised story of the flamboyant homosexual Quentin Crisp, played by John Hurt. The role won him a B.A.F.T.A. award as best actor of the year. (Thames)

Hollywood's Ann-Margret sang and danced in a lavish musical, **Ann-Margret Olsson**, one of ITV's shows with a ready market in other countries (ATV)

Akenfield, Peter Hall's sensitive film about a Suffolk village, made history by being shown simultaneously in the cinema and on ITV. It was part-financed by London Weekend.

Gerry and Sylvia Anderson employed their special effects experience, gained on puppet series such as **Thunderbirds,** to produce **Space 1999,** a lunar epic. (ATV)

213

1975

Carry On Laughing,
television version of
the cinema's
bold, box-office
romps. (ATV)

A thriller serial – a
comparative rarity
among TV series –
The Hanged Man
starred Colin Blakely
as a tough
construction company
boss. (Yorkshire)

A Place In Europe
showed famous
houses and palaces
where families still
live – including
Fontainebleau in
France. (Thames)

214

Jane Austen and Her World, a tribute to the author of **Emma** on the 200th anniversary of her birth. (Southern)

Derek Farr starred in **Nightingale's Boys,** a seven-part story about an elderly teacher who set out to discover what had become of the pupils from his class of 1949. (Granada)

The boom in nostalgia inspired **Get Some In,** a comedy series about RAF National Servicemen in the Fifties, with Tony Selby as a corporal. (Thames)

Graham Greene allowed his work to be televised for the first time in **Shades of Greene.** Donald Pleasence, John Le Mesurier and Bill Fraser starred in this one, **The Root of All Evil.** (Thames)

Comedian-turned-actor Bill Maynard played a widower with a roving eye in the comedy series, **The Life of Riley.** (Granada)

As comedies became more realistic, Rosemary Leach and Bernard Hepton starred as a couple frustrated by dull routine in a new domestic series, **Sadie, It's Cold Outside.** (Thames)

The documentary **Johnny Go Home** created nationwide concern with its revelation of what can happen to youngsters attracted by the lights of London. It was judged Best Factual Programme of 1975 by B.A.F.T.A. (Yorkshire)

Dr. No, first of six James Bond (Sean Connery) films acquired by ITV, caused a new wave of 007 fever with its small-screen showing. Discussions began about the need for extra time on television for interpreting the news and setting it in a wider context.

National Theatre Director Peter Hall became presenter of the arts magazine **Aquarius.**

In a year designated as International Women's Year, when a woman became IBA chairman, Margery Baker wrote and produced **A Place In Europe;** Andrea Wonfor produced **The First Train Now Arriving,** a documentary on the birth of railways; Jean Marsh was named the Variety Club's ITV personality for her part in creating, and performance in, **Upstairs, Downstairs;** ITN's Diana Edwards-Jones received an award for her direction of the 1974 General Election programmes, and the first products of Verity Lambert's 1974 appointment as Thames Television's Controller of Drama reached the screen.

1976

ITV approached its 21st Anniversary with a wider range than ever before, offering more news, current affairs, documentary, arts, religious and educational programmes. And it was still the most popular channel with the majority of viewers.

But the year was overshadowed by the uncertainty of "waiting for Annan"–the report of Lord Annan's Committee on the Future of Broadcasting.

Its recommendations are due to be considered by the Government in deciding on any changes in the structure of British television, including the allocation of the fourth channel. ITV argued that it needed this channel to enable it to compete with the BBC.

"A frustrating time," was how Lady Plowden, Chairman of the IBA, described this period.

Meanwhile, Harold Wilson handed over the Premiership to James Callaghan; Concorde entered regular service; and the sale of colour TV sets, which had slumped after the imposition of a 25 per cent VAT rate in 1975, was given new encouragement when Chancellor Denis Healey slashed the rate by half.

Luke's Kingdom was an "Australian Western" series about British settlers in New South Wales during the days of covered wagons.

1976

The International Pop Proms were devised by John Hamp, Head of Light Entertainment, to do for pop music what the Albert Hall Proms have done for the Classics. A 50-strong orchestra in the King's Hall, Manchester, backed international stars before an audience of 4,000. (Granada)

Life among the "never had it so good" working class was the theme of the comedy series **Yus My Dear,** with Arthur Mullard as a council house-dwelling bricklayer, Queenie Watts as his demanding wife. (LWT)

New star Marti Caine, a zany comedienne discovered on the **New Faces** talent show, won her own series, **Another Drop of Marti Caine.** (ATV)

Jack Parnell and his Orchestra have provided the backing music for many of ITV's spectacular shows. But with the current nostalgia for the sounds of the Forties, they took the limelight in **The Jack Parnell Big Band Show.** (ATV)

Hughie Green, who has presented talent shows on ITV since 1956, proved his own versatility by impersonating eight characters in **Hughie's Full House.** Here he joins the minstrels. (Thames)

1976

Clayhanger was a 26-part serial based on Arnold Bennett's trilogy of novels about family life in the Staffordshire Potteries during the latter part of the 19th century. Peter McEnery and Janet Suzman headed the cast of over 100. (ATV)

Destination America, a documentary in eight parts, told the story of Europeans who have emigrated to the New World in the past 150 years and helped to shape its character and destiny. (Thames)

1976

The Fortune Hunters,
adapted from a
West End of London
stage production,
starred Robert Morley
as a judge who had
to decide on a
disputed will. (Anglia)

Rock Follies, whose
style was adapted
from the Hollywood
musicals of the
Thirties, followed
three girl rock
singers in their
determined bid for
stardom. (Thames)

The Fosters was the first British situation comedy in which all the main characters were black. The series looked at the way a West Indian family coped with the pressures of life in London. (LWT)

Red Letter Day took turning points in its subjects' lives as a common theme. In Jack Rosenthal's **Ready when you are, Mr. McGill,** a film extra was given his first speaking role. (Granada)

1976

Richard Carpenter, creator of **Catweazle**, continued to place figures from the past in modern contexts with **The Ghosts of Motley Hall**, a series for children in which five historical spectres haunted a house together. (Granada)

The Feathered Serpent was an adventure series for children set in the Mexico of the Toltecs in 750 A.D. (Thames)

Following their successful series on BBC Radio, John Junkin, Tim Brooke-Taylor and Barry Cryer transferred the quickfire comedy show, **Hello Cheeky,** to television. (Yorkshire)

A lavish production of J. M. Barrie's **Peter Pan** starred the elfin Mia Farrow as Peter and Danny Kaye as a lively Captain Hook. (ATV)

227

Andrea Newman adapted her novel, **Bouquet of Barbed Wire,** for a TV series. It was the story of a man's obsessive love for his daughter – with Frank Finlay and Susan Penhaligon in the main roles – and audiences called for a sequel. (LWT)

The murder of Kenneth Lennon, who tipped-off the Special Branch about IRA activities in England, was reconstructed in the documentary, **Death of an Informer.** (ATV)

A team of climb turned cameramen Matterhorn, first filmed rec of an attempt the North Face. (H

Brian Young, Director General of the IBA since 1970, was knighted, and Sir Lew Grade received a life peerage.

ITV mourned the death of two of its most popular stars—Angela Baddeley, who played Mrs. Bridges in **Upstairs, Downstairs,** and Sidney James, of **Bless This House.**

Pat Phoenix, the popular Elsie Tanner in **Coronation Street,** returned to the serial after three years on the stage.

Alastair Burnet, for many years ITV's front man for big occasions, resigned the editorship of the Daily Express—a position he had held since 1974—and returned to the ITN team.

Joanna Lumley was chosen to be Patrick Macnee's co-star in a new series of **The Avengers.**

The Prince of Wales introduced **Prince Charles and Canterbury Cathedral** to aid an appeal for restoration funds.

Hughie Green presented his 400th. **Opportunity Knocks! Those Wonderful TV Times** was a quiz show about programmes and players in the 21 years of ITV.

THE ARTS

Television's arts programmes attract audiences which are small compared with those for light entertainment shows. But even a minority audience is large on television, and arts programmes are regularly watched by 2,000,000.

These large audiences are now prepared to enjoy operas and ballets on television although they might never travel to a live performance.

This is true in the regions and nationally. A Scottish Television production of Mahler's Eighth Symphony by the Scottish National Orchestra, in 1974, witnessed by 400,000 in the central Scottish region, compared with the 2,000 who could be seated in the hall in Glasgow.

ITV programmes have ranged from literature to music, painting to sculpture, and covered festivals from Edinburgh to Glyndebourne. ITV supports the arts and has made grants totalling £2,250,000 to regional associations and festivals.

Rudolf Nureyev and Nadia Nerina danced a Russian pas-de-deux, Laurencia, in **A Golden Hour,** a 90-minute programme from the Royal Opera House, Covent Garden, in 1964. (ATV)

THE ARTS

Leonide Massine's miracle play, **Laudes Evangelii,** was shown on Good Friday, 1961. (Associated-Rediffusion)

Also included in **A Golden Hour** in 1964 was an excerpt from **Tosca** by Maria Callas and Tito Gobbi. (ATV)

Elkan Allan's **Freedom Road** examined negro problems in music and song (Associated-Rediffusion). Sadler's Wells Opera Company presented Offenbach's opera **Orpheus in the Underworld.** (Granada)

THE ARTS

A production of Mozart's opera, **The Marriage of Figaro**, from Glyndebourne, was seen by 3,000,000 in 1973. (Southern)

Sir Geraint Evans,
a founder of Harlech
TV, was the star
of **Geraint Evans in
Covent Garden,** shown
in 1968. (Harlech)

THE ARTS

Artur Rubinstein gave
a farewell recital
of Saint-Saens' Piano
Concerto No. 2
in a 1976 edition of
Aquarius. (LWT)

Photographer David
Bailey's controversi
programme, **Warho**
about pop artist And
Warhol – gained hig
viewing figures. (A

Leonard Bernstein was
the conductor for
a 1971 performance of
The Verdi Requiem, by
The London Symphony
Orchestra. (LWT)

ITV was only available in certain areas when the first pop music craze – rock 'n roll and skiffle – swept Britain. This made little impact on television, which was geared to family entertainment.

But when the Beatles launched the second great pop music explosion in 1963, virtually every home had a record player and a television set. And teenagers had achieved great spending power, which made them a prime target for television advertisers.

Pop shows multiplied, and designers and directors outbid each other in the extravagance of their invention, using studio mist, split and multiple images, zooming and jerking cameras, with artists miming to their hit records.

But as the presentation grew more frenetic and teenagers favoured wilder sounds and increasingly outlandish appearances, older people were alienated and pop faded from television. Then, in the mid-Seventies, the musical gap narrowed: the middle-aged grew to like the same numbers as their children; youngsters started to appreciate music for its merit rather than decibel level and freak presentation.

Launching **Supersonic** in 1975, it's silver-haired producer, link man and director, Mike Mansfield, said: "Everybody's a teenager today." This policy, backed by the sounds of stars such as Alex Harvey, gave the series great impact. (LWT)

THE WORLD OF POP

Cool for Cats used a dance troupe in its interpretation of records in 1956. The disc jockey was Kent Walton. (ATV)

959, **Putting On
: Donegan** starred
ular jazz and
ffle guitarist Lonnie
negan. (ATV)

In 1959, Jack Good
sweetened pop when
he introduced violins
in **Boy Meets Girls;**
the boy of the title was
Marty Wilde (ABC).

A year earlier, Good
had presented ITV's
first pop show for
teenagers, **Oh Boy!**
with stars such as
Cliff Richard. (ABC)

THE WORLD OF POP

Jack Good's 1960 series was **Wham!!** the big beat sound featuring Joe Brown. Billy Fury was also in the series. (ABC)

The Beatles were among the celebrities in **Thank Your Lucky Stars,** which won the Melody Maker Top TV awards of 1962 and 1963. Bryan Matthew was the longest-serving compere on the show. (ABC)

Stars and Garters featured entertainers such as Tommy Bruce in a pub background (Associated-Rediffusion). The Top TV Show in the 1964 Melody Maker poll, **Ready, Steady Go**'s stars included Eric Burdon. (Associated-Rediffusion)

THE WORLD OF POP

Maggie Fitzgibbon
was hostess and singer
at **Maggie's Place** –
"the most swinging
night spot in town"–
in 1970. (LWT)

For a time the only
pop series on ITV,
the children's show,
Lift Off, was hosted
by the lovely Ayshea
Brough. (Granada)

The International Pop Proms accorded pop new status in 1976, moving it into the concert hall and using full concert orchestra backing to stars such as Brenda Arnau. (Granada)

SCHOOLS

ITV presented Britain's first television programmes for schools in 1957.

Only 80 schools in London and the Midlands watched the first programmes, and Associated-Rediffusion gave 100 sets to schools to encourage their use.

The first programmes were on immigrants, the International Geophysical Year, poetry, and job-opportunities. Since then the range has broadened and today nearly 30,000 schools – 80 per cent of the total – see the programmes.

The difficulty of fitting schools programmes into a curriculum was overcome in 1970, when videotape machines became widely available; ITV waived copyright restrictions to allow schools to tape series and show them as required. The making of schools programmes is the one area of TV in which ITV and the BBC work in close collaboration.

Seeing and Doing was a miscellany for six-year-olds (Thames). A production of **Romeo and Juliet,** for the 13 and over age group, starred David Weston and Jane Asher (Associated-Rediffusion). **Summing It Up** looked at mathematics in everyday life: this youngster was relating it to a model steam turbine (ATV). **Meeting Our Needs,** an integrated studies series, stimulated these pupils to make their own picks and shovels. (Yorkshire)

ADULT EDUCATION

Following the first schools programmes, there were regional experiments in adult education, notably a French language series by Associated-Rediffusion in 1960, and late night lectures on medicine, science, law and economics by Ulster Television in 1962.

Then the Government agreed to extra hours of television, provided they were used for adult education, and ITV presented Britain's first networked series in 1963. It was transmitted on Sunday mornings under the title **Sunday Session,** thus avoiding the word "education."

Since the first French and English series, the range has broadened enormously to cover subjects from car mechanics to sport, and many general programmes aim at broadening viewers' interests.

Drive-in, introduced by Shaw Taylor, featured subjects such as road safety, and encouraged the motorist to maintain his own car (Thames). Saving money was also the theme of **Kitchen Garden,** with Claire Rayner and Keith Fordyce showing how to get the best out of vegetables (Thames). D.I.Y. was again the aim of **Paint Along With Nancy,** presented by Nancy Kominsky. (HTV)

RELIGION

ITV pioneered the Sunday screening of religious programmes on television in 1956, after permission was obtained from the Postmaster General to show them in the early evening, a period when TV had been required to close to avoid affecting Church attendances.

The "closed period" has been used ever since for religious programmes, though they have gone on from simple discussions to include drama, satire and quizzes, and from representing the viewpoints of the main Christian denominations to examining esoteric faiths.

By the Seventies, however, opinion among many Church leaders had swung against a special enclave for religion, preferring that programmes should be scheduled on merit among those from other departments. And in 1976, the Central Religious Advisory Committee, which advises both ITV and the BBC on policy, agreed that the 6.15 to 7.25 pm period on Sundays need no longer be reserved exclusively for religion.

Weekday programmes, originally shown as epilogues, had already been moved to earlier times by some companies.

The other main area of religion on TV has been the outside broadcasts of Sunday morning church services. But in the mid-Seventies, these were interspersed with experimental studio programmes aimed at the uncommitted.

The first religious series transmitted in the Sunday evening "closed period" was **About Religion,** an early programme showing an interview with the late Cardinal John Heenan after he became the Roman Catholic Archbishop of Liverpool. (ATV)

RELIGION

Stars on Sunday presented religion with showbusiness flair and was the first "closed period" programme to break into the Top 20 charts. Big choirs were among the featured items. (Yorkshire)

Journey of a Lifetime showed John Bonney and Anne Lawson on their travels in the Holy Land (ABC). Dr. Donald Coggan, now Archbishop of Canterbury, was interviewed on the day of his enthronement as Archbishop of York. (Granada)

NEWS

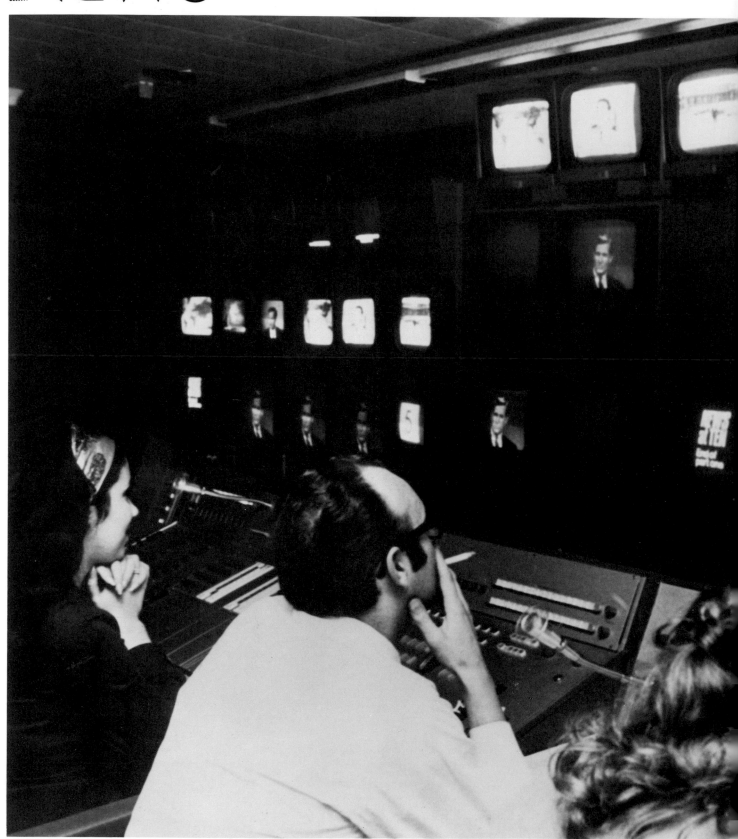

Television news in its current form was introduced to Britain by ITN. Up to the mid-Fifties, the news consisted of a bulletin read by an unseen announcer and illustrated mainly by photographs. But from the start, ITN used newscasters on screen, colloquial language, lively film reports and crisp interviews, and pursued scoops as enthusiastically as any daily newspaper.

Most innovations since then have come from ITN, which pioneered the peak hour 30-minute news on a major channel when it introduced **News at Ten** in 1967. ITN is a non profit-making company owned by the 15 programme companies. It has a staff of nearly 500, but can also draw on the news resources of the programme companies.

News at Ten is under way, and in the control room at ITN's headquarters, the director blends film reports and live coverage, videotape and graphics into a co-ordinated, half-hour programme.

NEWS

Soldiers and their families relax under guard in Ulster, the scene of ITN's longest-running story. Meanwhile, reporters range the world, and in Vietnam a bomb explodes near Michael Nicholson.

The largest schedu programmes mounted by ITN are on General Election nights, with 150 people in

studio, 20
tside Broadcast
ts, and 500
respondents who
ephone results.

In 1975, ITN covered
the dramatic moment
when Mrs. Sheila
Matthews was freed
at the end of the
Balcombe Street siege.

DOCUMENTARIES

Documentaries are to television what feature pages are to a newspaper. The range is wide – from the examination of a topical issue in a current affairs series, such as **This Week,** to a one-off programme like Kevin Billington's study of the Guards, **All the Queen's Men.**

From the £1 million budget **The World at War** to a regional programme providing a platform for a local pressure group; from **The Scientists** to **All Our Yesterdays** – if television is a window on the world, documentaries provide the furthest possible view.

Jonathan Dimbleby won an award named after his father, Richard Dimbleby, for **The Unknown Famine,** a **This Week** report about starvation in Ethiopia. The programme led to £5 million in aid being raised in Britain. (Thames)

DOCUMENTARIES

An interview with "Papa Doc" Duvalier, ruler of Haiti, won Alan Whicker the Dumont award for international journalism (Yorkshire). **The Royal Family,** made by a joint BBC/ITV consortium, has been shown twice on both networks.

The Struggle for Israel was a two-part history tracing the modern re-birth of the Jewish nation. (Yorkshire)

A **World in Action** team interviewed a Protestant Ulster Volunteer Force leader, missing from the prison where he had been serving a life sentence for murder. (Granada)

DOCUMENTARIES

A Buddhist monk cum gangleader was one of the surprises in **The Japanese Experience** (Yorkshire). **Too Long a Winter**, the story of a woman farming singlehanded in the Pennines, won an award from the Royal Television Society. (Yorkshire)

Bunny, the touching story of a five-year-old undergoing a new form of therapy for brain damage suffered from birth, was produced and directed by his fath Frank Cvitanovich. (Thames)

A camera team rode horses along trails high in the Peruvian Andes to find the mysterious Quechua tribe of Indians for the series, **The Disappearing World.** (Granada)

DOCUMENTARIES

Lee Lyon was killed by an elephant while filming a **Survival** programme in Africa; an award has been established in her memory (Anglia). Adrian Cowell spent two dangerous years filming in the Shan states of Burma for **Opium Warlords.** (ATV)

It's a Lovely Day Tomorrow was a dramatised documentary on the Second World War Bethnal Green tube disaster. (ATV)

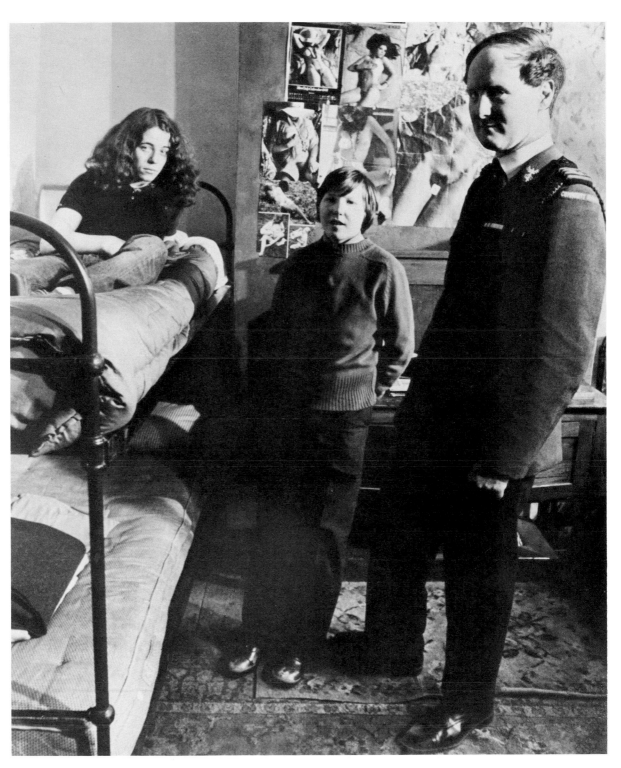

Johnny Go Home was a shock report about the voluntary organisation which preyed on young boys arriving homeless at London railway termini. It aroused a storm of feeling and public calls for strong action. (Yorkshire)

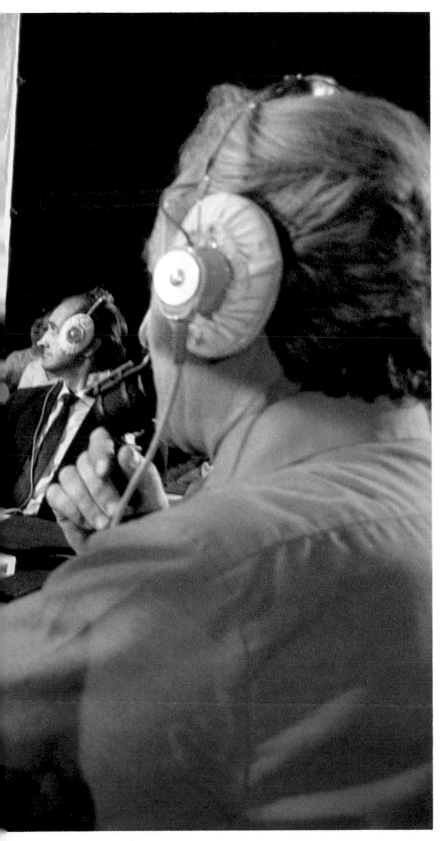

ITV has made a major contribution to today's techniques of sports coverage by pioneering the use of close-ups, instant replays and authoritative analysis by noted sportsmen. Professional commentators, such as John Rickman and Brian Moore, now rank among ITV's most popular personalities.

When ITV began, professional sport received little coverage because sports authorities feared its effects on attendances. Now, ITV offers an average of 10 hours of sport a week.

Big sports occasions – such as the FA Cup Final, championship fights and Classic horse races – receive massive viewing figures, but television has also increased the popularity of many minority sports.

Since 1965, ITV's coverage has been concentrated in **World of Sport,** a six-element, four-and-a half hour programme, to which many regional companies contribute. There is also a midweek programme of wrestling or football, apart from live coverage of other big events when they occur.

The popularity of professional wrestling, commentated since ITV's earliest days by Kent Walton, has been a television and social phenomenon. This tough, sometimes humorous, always exciting sport – and its many colourful characters – has become a traditional finale to **World of Sport.**

Two **International Sports Specials** are featured in each **World of Sport.** The second shows competition at its ultimate, including the World Team Speedway Championship.

usual events are
own in the first
ernational Sports
ecial, among them
e rough and tumble
ort of cyclocross.

SPORT

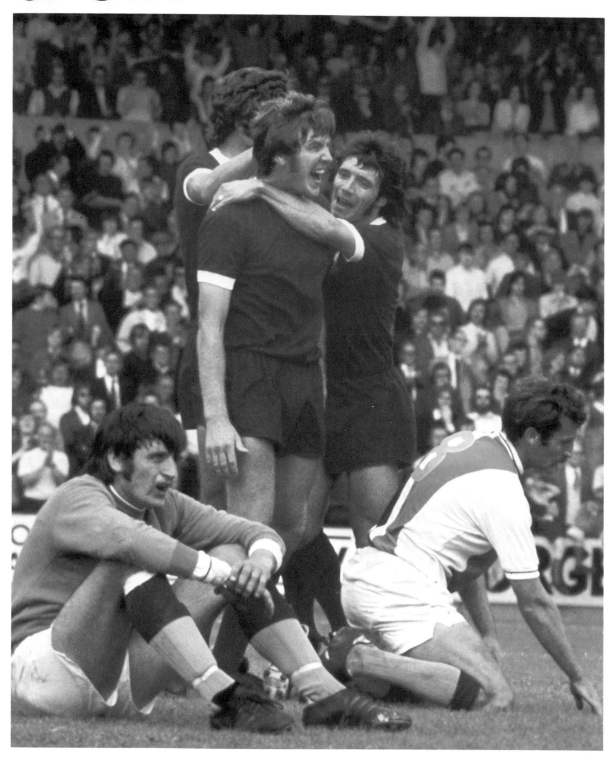

ITV's main emphasis is on football, with Saturday's League or Cup matches shown in regional programmes on Sunday afternoon.

Greyhound racing is one of the minority sports featured in **Sports Special One**, which made its first appearance in 1969

The crazy world of stock car racing is another of the off-beat events visited in **Sports Special One.** ITV's second emphasis is on horse racing, with **World of Sport** covering live 360 races a year.

World Championship
weightlifting is one
of the sports that
has been featured in
Sports Special Two.

ce Charles has
ped to popularise
o, and **World of**
rt awards a trophy
he best pony in
Coronation Cup.

Sports Special Two
has also included the
World Ski-ing Champ-
ionships and World
Series baseball.

273

THE DETECTIVES

Crime does pay – where television audiences are concerned. Although drama series have been made about newspapermen and nuns, doctors and farmers, they have been outnumbered by crime series, a staple part of ITV since it began. Heroes have included private detectives and secret agents and Scotland Yard's Fraud Squad. They have concerned crime in the Army (**Redcap**); in sport (**Crime Buster**); in America (**Columbo**); and in Holland (**Van der Valk**).

The trend has been towards realism. When ITV began, it inherited a fashion from mystery and thriller stories, in which private and amateur investigators were always smarter than policemen; in which senior police officers had to have titled relatives or work for fictitious departments. Lower ranks and country bobbies were figures of fun. Apart from big jewel robberies, the only crime worthy of investigation was murder.

Today, the private eye doesn't always make fools of the police, detectives work by method rather than intuition, and series concern real police departments. Police officers have problems outside the force and investigate petty as well as major crimes, while the growth of location filming has set crime in the streets, where most of it happens.

The Sweeney, a hardhitting series about the tough men of the Yard's Flying Squad, was filmed in the streets. The readers of TV Times voted the villain-loathing Chief-Insp. Regan, played by John Thaw, the Most Compulsive Male Character on ITV in 1976. (Thames)

THE DETECTIVES

International crime was the concern of Insp. Paul Duval, played by Charles Korvin, in **Interpol Calling**. (ATV)

Lockhart of the Yard, perhaps the most believable policeman of the Fifties, appeared in **Murder Bag, Crime Sheet** and finally **No Hiding Place**. Raymond Francis played him in all three series. (Associated-Rediffusion)

One-armed detective **Mark Saber** was played by Donald Gray, a real-life war hero idolised on both sides of the Atlantic (ATV). First of ITV's policeman heroes was **Colonel March of Scotland Yard,** with Boris Karloff. (ATV)

THE DETECTIVES

Elegance and tongue-in-cheek humour were the ingredients of **The Avengers,** with Patrick Macnee as an ultra-British secret agent and, successively, Honor Blackman, Diana Rigg (above), and Linda Thorson as partners. (ABC/Thames)

John Barrie played Sergeant Cork, a Victorian detective created by Lord Ted Willis in 1963. This inventive series looked at crime in the days before scientific methods of crime detection were available to the policeman. (ATV)

THE DETECTIVES

Public Eye's shabby Frank Marker, brilliantly played by Alfred Burke, made his debut in 1966. (ABC/Thames)

Gideon's Way, based on the hero of many John Creasey novels, starred John Gregson as Commander Gideon of the Yard. (ATV)

The Rat Catchers, about a small unit of British Intelligence, starred Gerald Flood, Philip Stone and Glyn Owen. (Rediffusion)

llan took life in
e cause of duty, but
ward Woodward
de him a
npathetic hero.
3C/Thames)

Patrick Mower was
one of the stars of the
Special Branch series,
which concerned the
subject of national
security (Thames).

Hunter's Walk
was about crime on a
smaller – but no
less dramatic – scale,
and featured a force
in the Midlands. (ATV)

THE COMEDIANS

Television comedy falls into two main categories: situation comedy – featuring actors such as John Alderton in **Please Sir!** – and the comedy show, starring a comic who may appear in sketches but retains his identity.

The latter are the successors to the stand-up comics of the variety halls. Variety was still popular when ITV began, and the biggest and starriest show was **Sunday Night at the London Palladium.** But variety, with individual acts introduced by a compere, has gradually given way to the comedy spectacular, in which the host acts, sings and clowns with his guests throughout the show.

The following pages recall some of ITV's most memorable comedians.

Double entendres, delivered with a sly smile, have been a popular feature of the long-running and highly successful series, **The Benny Hill Show.** (Thames)

THE COMEDIANS

Comediennes are rare, but Libby Morris became one of ITV's first comedy stars in **The Jack Jackson Show.** (ATV)

Tony Hancock starr as a night club owner in **Hancock's** the last of many series the comedia made for ITV. (ATV

The Morecambe and
Wise Show established
Eric and Ernie on TV,
and won them many
awards. (ATV)

Dave King starred in **The Dave King Show** in the Fifties (ATV). Tommy Trinder was the first compere of **Sunday Night at the** **London Palladium,** and once held the stage for 90 minutes when a power failure prevented scheduled transmission. (ATV)

Les Dawson, former Jack of all trades turned gloomy comic, was an **Opportunity Knocks!** discovery. He achieved his first series, **Sez Les**–a mixture of song, dance and lunacy–in 1969. (Yorkshire)

Larry Grayson rose
to stardom after he
presented his camp
humour in **Saturday
Variety** (ATV).
Youthful veteran

Max Bygraves began
a new line in popular
entertainment with
Singalongamax. (ATV)

THE COMEDIANS

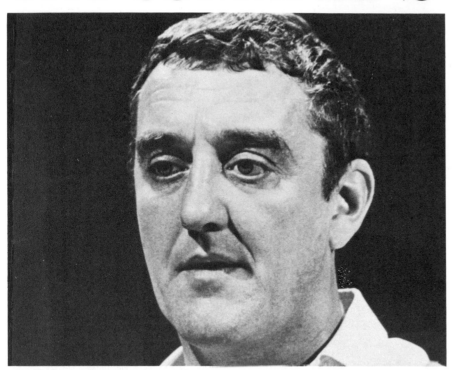

Jimmy Tarbuck found stardom as compere of **Sunday Night at the London Palladium** and was voted the Variety Club's Most

Promising Newcomer in 1965 (ATV). Actor and comedian Bernard Cribbins won his own show, **Cribbins,** in 1969. (Thames)

After several series of **The Charlie Drake Show,** the diminutive comic went on to star as an unemployable in **The Worker.** (ATV)

...d-haired singer
...d comic Ken Dodd–
...g of the Diddy
...–starred in his
...n series, **Doddy's**
...sic **Box**. (ABC)

THE COMEDIANS

Norman Wisdom
made his first situation
comedy series,
Norman, in 1970, but
wore his tight suit in
variety shows. (ATV)

Stanley Baxter was
regarded mainly as a
Scottish comedian –
until his remarkable
impressions were
accompanied by

casts and lavish
sets in **The Stanley
Baxter Picture
Show** in 1972. (LWT)

Tommy Cooper has had his ITV series since 1957, including the most recent, **The Tommy Cooper Hour** (Thames). Hosts of **Big Night Out** in the Sixties, the Winters had their own series, **Mike and Bernie's Scene.** (Thames)

CHILDREN

Children are voracious viewers, particularly 12 to 14-year-olds, who often watch for 24 hours a week. So all programmes before 9pm are intended for family viewing, although those designed for children are concentrated in the 90 minutes before the early evening news. These programmes, in one of the most scrutinised and controlled areas of television, account for nearly 10 hours a week. All ITV companies produce series for children, the output totalling as many as 40 a year, half of which are networked. Together they form a television service in miniature, blending entertainment, information and creative ideas in a range that varies from pop music and quizzes to natural history and kindergarten programmes.

The wide-ranging magazine **Magpie** has always encouraged an interest in worthwhile causes. In 1972, it showed **Breaking the Silence,** which led to young viewers raising £30,000 to buy teaching equipment for deaf children (Thames). **Black Arrow** was an adventure series based on the Robert Louis Stevenson story about the Wars of the Roses. (Southern)

CHILDREN

Children's fiction kept a jump ahead of space reality with **Pathfinders to Mars,** starring Gerald Flood (ABC). **Biggles** was made while W. E. Johns was still writing best-selling stories for boys, and featured the flying detective. (Granada)

The Adventures of **William Tell,** with Conrad Phillips as the Swiss hero, was a successor to **Robin Hood.** (ATV)

sea-going replica
the Golden Hind
s reconstructed for
Francis Drake,
h Terence Morgan
Drake. (ATV/ABC)

Answers to thousands
of questions have been
demonstrated in **How**
(Southern). **Romper
Room** was developed
from an American

kindergarten series
and adapted by many
ITV companies. Here,
Anglia Television's
version is presented
by Rosalyn Thompson.

CHILDREN

The science fiction
series **Timeslip** sent
a group of children
leaping ahead to
the year 1990. (ATV)

Redgauntlet was an
eight-part adaptation
of the novel by Sir
Walter Scott, set in
18th century Dumfries
(Scottish). **The Wind**
in the Willows was
the first illustrated
version of a famous
story for children,
with narration by John
Worsley. (Anglia)

llyfoot – whose
eme was in the Top
–centred on a
ing stable and was
spired by Monica
ckens. (Yorkshire)

In **Clapperboard,** a
series dealing with
many aspects of the
cinema, Derek Ware
showed how a stunt-
man falls. (Granada)

PUPPETS

Puppets have played a big role in entertaining children. The range has covered the simplest of glove puppets to sophisticated £300 models on wires one five-thousandth of an inch thick.

With lips synchronised electronically to sound tracks pre-recorded by well-known actors, these miniature marvels have become TV stars in their own right.

Thunderbirds brought puppets to a peak of sophistication and popularity and won a Television Society silver medal for outstanding work in 1966 (ATV). Appealing versions of stories such as **Colditz** and **Treasure Island** were presented in Michael Bentine's **Potty Time,** which employed 18in. high puppets (Thames). Following **Thunderbirds,** Gerry and Sylvia Anderson produced **Joe 90,** a nine-year-old boy transformed into a secret agent. (ATV)

PUPPETS

Romantic novelist Roberta Leigh created **Torchy,** a battery-powered little boy, in 1960 (Associated-Rediffusion). Jean Morton presented two puppet koala bears in **The Tingha and Tucker Club.** (ATV)

Small Time's Wally Whyton sang, played and talked to Pussy Cat Willum. (Associated-Rediffusion)

ppet pigs **Pinky**
d Perky mimed the
trumentalists
ainst a pop music
ckground. (Thames)

Glove puppeteer
Harry Corbett threw
custard pies in
his own face for **The**
Sooty Show (Thames).
Underwater characters
such as this one
were created by Gerry
and Sylvia Anderson
for their submarine
saga, **Stingray.** (ATV)

ITV introduced top-rating American programmes to Britain in its first week, screening **I Love Lucy** and **Dragnet.** Their slick style and professional gloss made an immediate impact.

ITV's schedules have contained American programmes ever since, although the IBA's rule is that a week's viewing must not include more than 14 per cent of foreign material.

Westerns were an obvious choice because they could not be made in Britain. Crime series remain perennially popular and dramatic serials, such as **Peyton Place,** have won big audiences.

Until a few years ago, American series – like British ones – were normally 30 minutes or one-hour long. But Hollywood now produces made-for-television films, such as **Columbo** and **Banacek,** which are of 90 minutes duration.

Angie Dickinson, here with Earl Holliman, was Pepper Anderson, a glamorous girl with a gun in her handbag, in the series **Police Woman.** After **The Six Million Dollar Man** came **The Bionic Woman,** a 60 mph blonde played by Lindsay Wagner. And up from New Mexico came **McCloud** (Dennis Weaver), a deputy marshal who was assigned to the New York Police in **Mystery Movies.**

HOLLYWOOD ON TV

I Love Lucy earned a fortune for Lucille Ball, the dizzy heroine of this highly successful domestic comedy series.

Burly Brod Crawford handed out homilies as well as justice in his role of Capt. Dan Mathews, **Highway Patrol**'s toughest cop.

James Arness was Marshal Matt Dillon in both **Gun Law** and **Gunsmoke,** while Jack Webb wrote, produced and directed **Dragnet,** and also played the laconic Sergeant Joe Friday in the series.

HOLLYWOOD ON TV

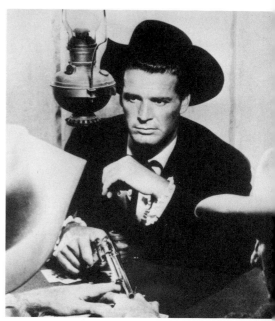

Wagon Train tracked the pioneers of the West on their journey from Missouri to California, and featured Ward Bond.

Introduced by the master director in person, **The Alfred Hitchcock Hour** presented a series of chilling suspense stories. James Garner was a Wester gambler, who was also an ace with a gun, in **Maverick.**

wkeye and the Last
he Mohicans was
sed on the James
himore Cooper novel
out the Anglo/
nch war in Canada.

77 Sunset Strip
featured Kookie (Ed
Byrnes) as one of
a team of detectives
operating in the
night club quarter of

Hollywood. That city
was also home to
Popeye, but after 25
years as a movie
star, he began a new
career on TV.

Clint Eastwood and
Eric Fleming starred
as small ranchers
from Texas, driving
their cattle to a
railhead, in **Rawhide**.

me Greene ran the
nderosa ranch with
three devoted,
hard-hitting
ns in **Bonanza**. Ben
sey was a more

idealistic hero, a
neurosurgeon, played
by Vincent Edwards.

Naked City was a
crime series, filmed
mainly in New York,
with Paul Burke
as a police officer.

HOLLYWOOD ON TV

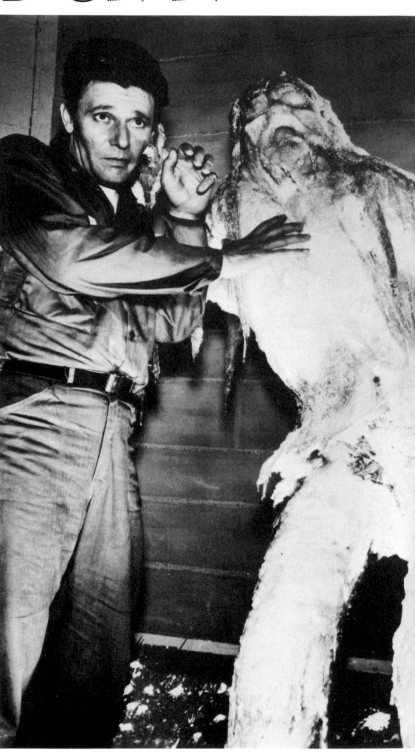

Voyage to the Bottom of the Sea featured a futuristic nuclear submarine. Also aimed at younger viewers, **The Forest Rangers** dealt with game control and firefighting in the wilds of Canada.

The Outer Limits was a series of disturbing science fiction fantasies that began with the warning: "Do not be alarmed!"

The **Flintstones** and **Yogi Bear** were two products to emerge from Joe Barbera and Bill Hanna's giant cartoon film factory.

Buddy Ebsen starred as the head of an oil-rich family of yokels sampling Hollywood in **The Beverly Hillbillies.**

HOLLYWOOD ON TV

Barbara Stanwyck starred as a widow running a ranch in **The Big Valley.** Charles Addams' New Yorker cartoons came to television when his macabre characters appeared in a comedy series, **The Addams Family.**

David Janssen was a hunted man in **The Fugitive,** a series that gained a regular following with its cliffhanger endings.

Peyton Place, based
on the novel by Grace
Metalious about life
in a small American
town, also proved
addictive in Britain.

HOLLYWOOD ON TV

Chicago in the 1920s
was the setting for
The Untouchables, with
Robert Stack as Eliot
Ness, the man who
fought the mobsters.

A 300lb. dolphin
played the title role
in **Flipper,** the
story of two small
boys and their clev
but unusual pet.

J. Edgar Hoover was the adviser on **FBI**, which starred Efrem Zimbalist Jr. as a G-man. A less conventional crimebuster was **Batman**, played by Adam West, whose superhuman powers thwarted the crooks of five continents.

HOLLYWOOD ON TV

Mission Impossible featured the husband and wife team of Martin Landau and Barbara Bain in the role of undercover agents. The comedy stars of **Hogan's Heroes** were Americans in a German P.O.W. camp, who found no mission impossible....

Tarzan, the jungle hero of numerous films, came to television in a series starring Ron Ely.

Flying saucer stories inspired **The Invaders**, in which Roy Thinnes played an architect trying to convince the world that aliens were landing. Bill Cosby was one of the first black actors to star in a TV series, appearing alongside Robert Culp in **I Spy**.

A force of former
jailbirds operating
as commandos behind
German lines was
the subject of
Garrison's Gorillas.

Name of the Game,
of the first 90 minute
made-for-television
movies, featured G
Barry as a multi-
millionaire publishe

The hero of **Marcus Welby MD** was an unfashionable figure in modern America – a G.P., played by veteran Robert Young.

Banacek starred George Peppard as a freelance claims investigator making a rich living from insurance companies.

Cade's County was a modern Western, with Glenn Ford as a jeep-riding sheriff.

Sesame Street used modern advertising techniques in an educational series aimed at children of pre-school age.

A situation comedy series, **The New Dick Van Dyke Show** featured the star as host of a talk show. Elizabeth Montgomery played Samantha, a pretty housewife who was able to cast spells, in **Bewitched.**

HOLLYWOOD ON TV

Fascinating locations were the backdrops for two slick crime series–**Hawaii Five-O,** starring Jack Lord, and **Streets** **of San Francisco,** featuring Karl Malden as a volatile but likeable detective.

In the wake of kara films came **Kung F** with David Carradi as a monk who fou like a windmill.

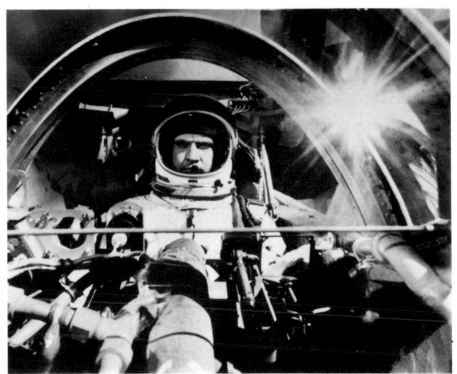

The Six Million Dollar Man (Lee Majors) was a crashed test pilot rebuilt as a bionic superman. Romance was mixed with investigation in **McMillan and Wife,** starring Rock Hudson as a suave police commissioner, Susan St. James as his wife.

Peter Falk gave a
brilliant performance
as **Columbo**, a police
lieutenant whose
diffidence concealed
an agile mind.

ch Man, Poor Man,
win Shaw's novel
anning the 30 post-
r years, became a
mpelling 12-hour
serial in 1976.

COMMERCIALS

ITV's commercials make the service possible; 98 per cent of its income is derived from the sale of advertising time, limited to a daily average of not more than six minutes in an hour.

The first commercials had an immediate and startling impact. Advertisers' slogans were quoted like comedians' catchphrases and jingles were sung and whistled. The novelty has gone, but many commercials are still highly enjoyed as entertainment, which is not surprising, since some of the best film directors, songwriters and actors produce them. There are nearly 22,000 new commercials every year, most of them regional advertisements consisting of simple slides. But another 7,000 come from national advertisers.

Because of their impact, the ITA–as it was then–evolved a tight system of controls, banning the advertising of some products and services and imposing a list of commandments on the remainder. These were stricter than any the advertising industry had ever known and reacted on the industry as a whole, so that it set up similar codes of practice.

Four stars of ITV commercials: actress Mary Holland, who has played Katie, the Oxo housewife, since 1959; a big dog who patronises a small man in the Kennomeat cartoons; Arthur the cat (died 1976), who scooped up Kattomeat with his paw, and William Franklyn, seen for many years in the Schweppes commercials.

COMMERCIALS

Almost-human chimps
have starred for
Brooke Bond PG Tips.
An American-style
technique created
the Tic-Tac detective.

A speedboat crashed
into a lakeside
chalet in a James
Bond-style stunt for
Fabergé after shave.

e sexy voices and
ltry glances of
e lovely girls who
vertised Manikin
gars affronted some
omen's libbers...

The puppet Tivvy
promoted TV Times in
the Sixties, while
women found the man
who smoked St. Bruno
was irresistible.

THE REGIONS

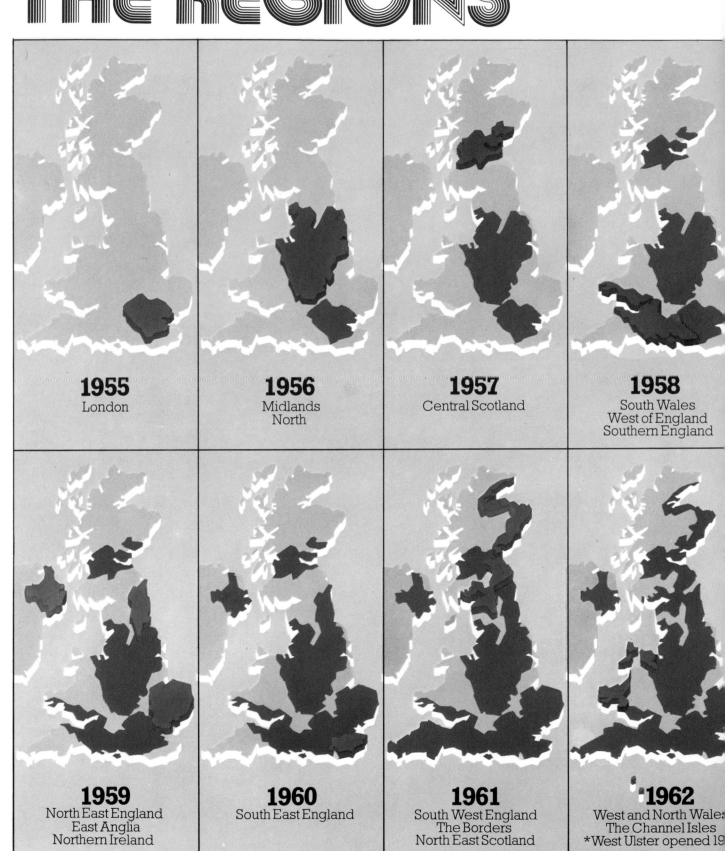

1955
London

1956
Midlands
North

1957
Central Scotland

1958
South Wales
West of England
Southern England

1959
North East England
East Anglia
Northern Ireland

1960
South East England

1961
South West England
The Borders
North East Scotland

1962
West and North Wales
The Channel Isles
*West Ulster opened 19

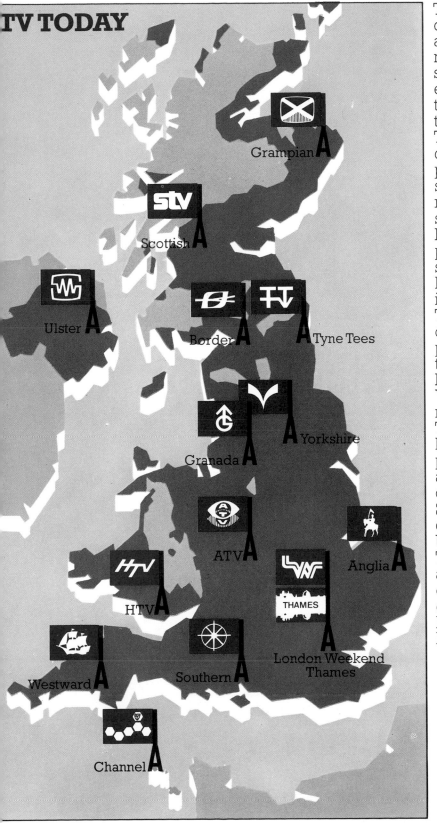

TV TODAY

Grampian

STV
Scottish

Ulster

Border

Tyne Tees

Yorkshire

Granada

ATV

HTV

Anglia

THAMES

London Weekend
Thames

Westward

Southern

Channel

Two-thirds of ITV's total production is of programmes made specifically for and about individual regions. This is made possible by ITV's unique federal structure, based on 14 regional areas, each with a programme company – two in London – responsible for everything transmitted in that area.

This coverage stemmed from ITV's original reception area in London and parts of the Home Counties. Relatively small as this was in 1955, it rapidly mushroomed to nationwide proportions, as shown in the series of maps on the left. ITV's structure is more costly in manpower and money than a centralised system, but it diversifies control, stimulates competition, and helps to generate ideas and opportunities.

The 15 programme companies, including London's, all produce regional programmes. In practice, however, the five "central" companies – Thames, London Weekend, ATV, Granada and Yorkshire – concentrate on providing nationally networked programmes.

The other 10 companies, while contributing to the network, concentrate on programmes reflecting life in their areas. Five are classed as large regional companies – Anglia, HTV, Scottish, Southern and Tyne Tees; the others, classed as small, are Border, Grampian, Ulster, Westward and Channel.

They produce regional news magazines and programmes ranging from local consumer affairs to politics and light entertainment. And audiences for these local interest programmes are often larger than for networked shows.

Two of a Kind talked
to legless war hero
Douglas Bader and
Marilyn Gillies, who
was born without
arms (Grampian). The

Selkirk Casting of
the Colours, which
commemorates a
survivor of Flodden,
was shown in
About Britain. (Border)

What Price Oil?
was an examination
of the effects on
North East Scotland
of oil exploration
offshore. It won an

S.F.T.A. Shell award
for an outstanding
contribution to the
understanding of
trade and industry
in 1973. (Grampian)

Bygones has shown old craftsmen passing on their skills and lore (Anglia). **The Stag-hunters** rode with the Devon and Somerset Stag Hounds at the time of a controversial move to outlaw stag hunting. (Westward)

They'll Never Get It To Fly, a history of helicopters, asked Prince Philip about his experiences as a pilot (Westward).

Prince Charles, who also flies "choppers," was more concerned with rural life when he met a Welsh farmer in **Countryside.** (HTV)

The Dame of Sark talked about life on her feudal island in a programme made shortly before her death (Channel).

Aubrey Buxton devised, edited and presented the nature programme, **Countryman.** (Anglia)

Country Boy, Jack Hargreaves introduced a 14-year-old Londoner to the country. (Southern). **The Living Wall,** a net-worked documentary, followed the author Hunter Davies on his trek along Hadrian's Wall. (Tyne Tees/Border co-production)

Westward Television contributed news coverage to ITN when the giant Torrey Canyon oil tanker went aground off Cornwall. **Big Jack's Other World** was a portrait of the North East soccer idol, Jack Charlton. (Tyne Tees)

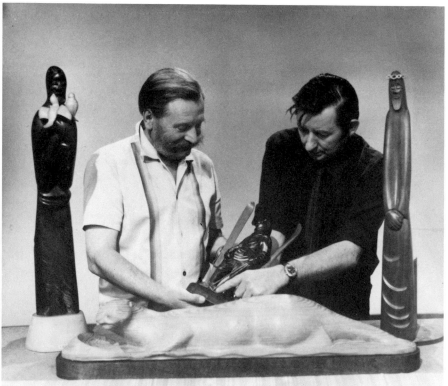

In **Hobby Horse,** Alick Cleaver looked at hobbies – such as wood carving – pursued in the region (Border). **Houseparty,** an afternoon programme for women, has celebrated more than 1,000 shows. (Southern)

Midnight Oil was a university of the air, produced in conjunction with Queen's University, Belfast (Ulster). **Regional**

Flavour looked at th dishes of ITV region this one with chef Toni Stoppani and folklore expert Emil Redmond. (Border)

Spectrum, a review of local arts, welcomed guests such as author Frederick Forsyth (Ulster). **Flashpoint,** a current affairs series, began when trouble grew in the Province in 1967. (Ulster)

THE REGIONS

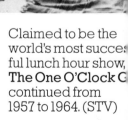

John Cairney played Scotland's national poet in a six-part serial, **A Man Called Burns** (STV). After the formation of the

Scottish Opera in 1962, Ian Wallace introduced opera to newcomers in **Singing for Your Supper.** (STV)

Glyndebourne, the Sussex country home of opera, has been visited several times for programmes by Southern Television.

Claimed to be the world's most succes ful lunch hour show, **The One O'Clock C** continued from 1957 to 1964. (STV)

Dr. Price 1800–1893 starred William Squire as a bizarre 19th century doctor. (HTV). **Thick as Thieves,** a crime drama with Leonard Rossiter, won a Royal Television Society Pye Best Regional Production award in 1972. (HTV)

THE REGIONS

Mary Slessor was the story of a Dundee missionary who went to Nigeria to devote herself to the people of Calabar (Grampian).

The Bitter Years was a documentary about German rule in the Channel Isles during the Second World War. (Channel)

A Dog's Life at the Rising Sun was a documentary about the Geordie world of whippet racing. (Tyne Tees)

340

e documentary **oggs VC** examined e heroism of the egendary coxswain Cromer lifeboat. nglia)

341

A Magnificent Man and His Flying Machines was the story of 19th century aviation pioneer Sir George Cayley (Anglia).

The Loss of the SS Schiller re-created the tragedy off the Scilly Isles in 1875. (Westward)

Wyvern at War told the story of the 43rd (Wessex) Division of territorial infantry from D Day, 1944, to VE Day in 1945. Using the fighting men's own words, it won an American Emmy award. (Westward)

The First Train Now Arriving was a dramatised documentary celebrating the 150th anniversary of George Stephenson – played by Bryan Pringle – the father of railways. (Tyne Tees)

Further details of actors and characters pictured throughout this book.

1971

168/169 **Upstairs, Downstairs :** Pauline Collins (Sarah), Angela Baddeley (Mrs. Bridges), George Innes (Alfred), Gordon Jackson (Mr. Hudson), Evin Crowley (Emily), Brian Osborne (Pearce), Patsy Smart (Roberts), Jean Marsh (Rose). Foreground: David Langton (Richard Bellamy), Rachel Gurney (Lady Marjorie Bellamy).
170/171 **Persuasion :** Richard Vernon (Admiral Croft), Bryan Marshall (Capt. Wentworth).
172/173 **And Mother Makes Three :** David Parfitt (Peter), Wendy Craig (Sally Harrison), Robin Davies (Simon). **The Persuaders :** Roger Moore (Lord Brett Sinclair), Tony Curtis (Danny Wilde).
174/175 **Bless This House :** Sidney James (Sid Abbott), Diana Coupland (Jean Abbott), Sally Geeson (Sally), Robin Stewart (Mike). **The Fenn Street Gang :** Peter Cleall (Eric Duffy), Leon Vitali (Peter Craven), Peter Denyer (Dennis Dunstable), Carol Hawkins (Sharon Eversleigh), Liz Gebhardt (Maureen Bullock), David Barry (Frankie Abbott), Foreground : Jill Kernan (Penny Hedges), John Alderton (Bernard Hedges).

1972

178/179 **Country Matters – The Higgler :** Keith Drinkel.
180/181 **The Strauss Family :** Stuart Wilson (Strauss Jr.). **Van der Valk :** Barry Foster (Van der Valk), Michael Latimer (Kroon). **My Good Woman :** Leslie Crowther (Clive Gibbons), Sylvia Syms (Sylvia Gibbons).
182/183 **Black Beauty :** Judi Bowker (Vicky). **Who Do You Do? :** Peter Goodwright, Freddie Starr. **Sale of the Century** (Celebrity edition) : Arthur Askey, Nicholas Parsons, Sheila Hancock, Jennifer Cresswell, John Alderton. **Shut That Door :** Tessie O'Shea, Larry Grayson. **Love Thy Neighbour :** Kate Williams (Joan Booth), Jack Smethurst (Eddie Booth), Nina Baden-Semper (Barbara Reynolds), Rudolph Walker (Bill Reynolds).
184/185 **Adam Smith :** Andrew Keir (Adam).
186/187 **Emergency – Ward 10 :** John Carlisle and Charles Lamb. **Emmerdale Farm :** Andrew Burt (Jack Sugden), Frazer Hines (Joe Sugden).

1973

190/191 **Long Day's Journey Into Night :** Laurence Olivier (James Tyrone). **Shabby Tiger :** John Nolan (Nick Faunt), Prunella Gee (Anna Fitzgerald). **Beryl's Lot :** Mark Kingston (Tom Humphries), Carmel McSharry (Beryl Humphries).
192/193 **Divorce His : Divorce Hers :** Richard Burton, Elizabeth Taylor (Martin and Jane Reynolds).
194/195 **The Brontes of Haworth :** Michael Kitchen (Branwell Bronte), Ann Penfold (Anne Bronte), Alfred Burke (The Rev. Patrick Bronte), Freda Dowie (Aunt Branwell), Rosemary McHale (Emily), Vickery Turner (Charlotte Bronte).
196/197 **Sam :** John Price (Alan Dakin), Ray Smith (George Barraclough), Barbara Ewing (Dora Wilson), Alethea Charlton (Ethel Barraclough), Kevin Moreton (Sam). **Helen – A Woman of Today :** Diana Hutchinson (Diana Tulley), Christopher Ballantyne (Chris Tulley), Martin Shaw (Frank Tulley), Alison Fiske (Helen Tulley).

1974

200/201 **Intimate Strangers :** Anthony Bate (Harvey Paynter), Patricia Lawrence (Joan Paynter). **Thick As Thieves :** Bob Hoskins (Dobbs), Pat Ashton (Annie), John Thaw (Stan). **The Inheritors :** Peter Egan (Michael Gethin), Robert Urquhart (James, Lord Gethin).
202/203 **Boy Dominic :** Richard Todd (Charles Bulman).
204/205 **The Zoo Gang :** Lilli Palmer (Manouche Roget), John Mills (Tommy Devon), Barry Morse (Alec Marlowe), Brian Keith (Stephen Halliday). **South Riding :** Norman Scace (Rev. Millward Peckover), Barbara Ogilvie (Miss Parsons), Dorothy Tutin (Miss Sarah Burton, MA), Clive Swift (Councillor Alfred Ezekiel Huggins).
206/207 **Rising Damp :** Frances de la Tour (Miss Jones), Don Warrington (Philip Smith), Richard Beckinsale (Hallam), Leonard Rossiter (Rigsby). **Wheeltappers and Shunters Social Club :** Colin Crompton.

1975

210/211 **My Brother's Keeper :** George Layton (Brian Booth), Jonathan Lynn (Pete Booth). **Born Free :** Diana Muldaur and Elsa. **The Stars Look Down :** Ian Hastings (David Fenwick), Susan Tracey (Jenny Sunley).
212/213 **Akenfield :** Ronald Blythe (Vicar), Lyn Brooks (Charlotte Rouse), Garrow Shand (Tom Rouse). **Space 1999 :** Anthony Valentine (alien).
214/215 **Carry On Laughing :** Kenneth Connor, Jack Douglas, Joan Sims. **The Hanged Man :** Colin Blakely (Lew Burnett). **A Place in Europe :** the house and gardens of Vaux-le-Vicomte.

1976

218/219 **Luke's Kingdom :** Oliver Tobias (Luke Firbeck).
220/221 **Yus My Dear :** Arthur Mullard (Wally Briggs), Queenie Watts (Lil Briggs).
222/223 **Clayhanger :** Janet Suzman (Hilda Lessways), Peter McEn (Edwin Clayhanger).
224/225 **Rock Follies :** Rula Lenska (Q), Charlotte Cornwell (Anna), Julie Covington (Dee). **The Fosters :** Lenny Henry (Sonny), Carmen Munro (Vilma), Isabelle Lucas (Pearl), Norman Beaton (Samuel), Lawrie Mark (Benjamin), Sharon Rosita (Shirley). **Red Letter Day :** Jack Shepherd (Phil, the Director), Joe Black (Joe McGill).
226/227 **The Ghosts of Motley Hall :** Nicholas le Prevost (Fanny), Arthur English (Bodkin), Sean Flanagan (Matt), Freddie Jones (Sir George Uproar), Sheila Steafel (The White Lady). **The Feathered Serpent :** Patrick Troughton (Nas), Diané Keen (Chimalma). **Hello Cheeky :** John Junkin, Barry Cryer, Tim Brooke-Taylor.
228/229 **Bouquet of Barbed Wire :** Frank Finlay (Peter Manson), Susan Penhaligon (Prue Sorenson). **Death of An Informer :** Tom Bell (Kenneth Lennon).

347

Published by Independent Television Publications Limited

Executive Editor Peter Jackson: Editor Anthony Davis: Associate Editor Les Pipe: Assistant Editor Colin Ellson: Researchers Philippa Clarke, Peter Harwood, Gill Hutchinson, Lynn Walford, George Whitnall: Art Director Stanley Glazer: Designer Malcolm Gipson: Design Assistants Aean Pinhero, Francesca Wilkinson: Picture Research Ted Nunn: Picture Research Assistants Mike Hills, Eddie Pedder, Pamela Finch, Glenn Skinner: Additional Picture Research Jack Breckon (Thames), Doreen Challis (LWT), Dave Dawson (Anglia), Frank Duesbury (ITN), Brian Jeeves (Yorkshire), Rosemary Kent (ITN), Barry Ledingham (ATV), Fiona Nightingale (Granada), Frances Pardell (ITC), Bob Simmons (HTV West), Laurie Taylor (Tyne Tees), Simon Theobalds (Southern): TVTimes photographs by Peter Bolton, Derry Brabbs, Roderick Ebdon, Bernard Fallon, Bert Hill, Ron McFarlane, Ted Nunn, John Paul, Roger Scruton, Paul Stokes: Contributing Photographers Chris Bonington, Ron Coburn, Gerry Cranham, Stewart Darby, Reginald Davis, Dave Dawson, Dick Dawson, Tony Duffy, Dave Farrell, Phil King, Leo Mason, Jack Moody, Tony Nutley, Stuart Sadd, John Silverside, Ian Vaughan, George Wiggins, Jack Wiggins: Contributing Photographic Agencies Colorsport, Popperfoto, Press Association: Monochrome Presentation Sevrin Elder, Bert Husk, Ian Martin, Alan Morris, Ann Robinson: Regional maps by Diagram.